Manag... Self !

It's only your mind we're talking about, oh... *and* your relationships, *and* your life.

Understanding WHY and HOW to convert your crazy into confidence and success, both within yourself and in your relationships.

Art by Shawn K. Carson

Library of Congress Cataloging-in-Publication Data

Guttenberger, Randy
Managing Your Crazy Self / Randy Guttenberger

ISBN: 978-0-692-60390-1

Key words: communication, improve relationships, how to manage
others, stress, behavior, emotions, success.

Ceros, Inc. www.cerosinc.com; randy@cerosinc.com

Editors
Kim Andrews
Michael Carr

Associate Editor
Marilyn Anderson

Guttenberger Press
Houston, Texas

Client Testimonials

"You figured me out in two sessions! How? I spent decades in therapy. Randy, I walked on hot burning coals! Two times—10 feet and 15 feet! No one told me what you saw in just two sessions! Walking on coals didn't solve my problems. You did. I have my life back."
—Jackie H., Realtor

"I almost fired a good employee because I didn't know how to manage them. That employee is still with me 14 years later."
—Sergio B., Chief Nurse Officer

"You helped me give myself permission to love myself, and showed me how to think in healthy ways."
—Beth T., Administrator

"You give me a read on my staff that would have taken me six months to learn on my own."
—Jon Li M., CEO

"I learned more from you in two or three sessions than in years of therapy."
—Marilyn A., HR Director

"Why isn't anyone teaching this? I wish I had learned this long ago."
—Gregg S., COO

"I look back five years ago and see what I have accomplished from your coaching. I never would have known. Thank you for your insights and direction."
—Jackie K., Geophysicist

"You helped me see my troubles and made me feel that I can manage them. It makes all the difference. I have even restored broken relationships with my extended family."
—Maria G., Area SR VP

"Randy, you put the whole package together: mind, personality traits, experiences, goals. Everything makes sense."
—Jon Lee M., IT Director

"I am not sure what you said to my son, but he went from flunking out of college and not talking to us to walking with a spine in his back. Now he openly tells us his problems."
—Bob R., Psychiatrist

"Randy, thank you for helping me with my staff. Even more surprising to me, my family says I am better."
—Marion J., CFO

The above are actual client responses. Names have been changed to protect confidentiality.

Acknowledgments

Several authors have provided me with wonderful insights on how managing thoughts and emotions can bring personal peace of mind and result in healthy relationships. I am eternally grateful to have discovered their work, and have used their concepts successfully for decades in my coaching in corporations and with individuals. This book is my creative expression of bringing these concepts together in a fun, simple, memorable, and effective way so that others can apply them and achieve success in their lives.

Bill Crawford, Life from the Top of the Mind

Harville Hendrix, Getting the Love You Want

John Bradshaw, Bradshaw On: The Family

Elizabeth Brown, Living Successfully with Screwed-Up People

Tara Bennett-Goleman, *Emotional Alchemy*

Bill Bonnstetter, Judy Suiter, and Randy Widrick, *The Universal Language DISC: A Reference Manual*

Special Acknowledgments

My greatest thanks go to my parents, Paul and Willene Guttenberger, for all the years of support and encouragement. Words cannot express my appreciation enough, but here they are: I love you.

My sons Ben, Jon, and Nic have my heartfelt appreciation for the inspiration and many insights they have given me. Many blessings on you. I can't imagine what it's like to have a behavioral analyst as a father. But I am eternally grateful to be that guy.

I want to thank Bill Bonnstetter, founder of Target Training International, for his vision, passion, and persistence in his work, and for encouraging me to pursue my own.

Thanks to my great friend Bob Goldstein, for his boundless humor and thought-provoking conversations, for allowing me to be me while challenging my own thoughts, and for sharing his insights, which helped me discover mine.

My deepest thanks to Marilyn Anderson for her hours of editing, patience, and humor. Without your help, I might still be talking about writing a book someday.

To Jeff Holland, hospital CEO, my endless gratitude for his linguistic wit and for allowing me to work with his teams for almost two decades. Jeff believed in me and introduced me to his best people, many of whom invited me to continue to be part of their journey over the years.

To Bill Crawford, for bringing the *Life from the Top of the Mind* principles to my life.

To Shawn Carson, a wonderfully creative talent, for his genius at rendering abstract concepts in graphic form. Your art is truly a gift of God's creativity.

Visit www.managingyourcrazyself.com to:

- Receive special offers.
- View short videos covering topics such as improving relationships, communication tips, and much more.
- View the calendar for upcoming workshops.
- Inquire about hosting a workshop.
- Use your rhino mind and take charge of your life!
- Register for updates, newsletters, blogs, and videos.

If you are interested in becoming an associate or distributor for Ceros, Inc., email me at randy@cerosinc.com.

CEROS, INC

Mission Statement

To bring out the best in people,

often when they can't see it in themselves,

by providing tools and insights for their success.

No ostriches or rhinos were harmed
in the production of this book.

Contents

Contents vii

Preface ix

Introduction..1

A Five-Step Journey to Renew Your Mind 7

Understanding the Structure of Your Mind

Chapter 1 Meet the Ostrich and the Rhino...................................11

Chapter 2 The Physical Structure of Your Brain:
  A Blueprint..13

Chapter 3 The Instinctive Brain Begins with the Limbic System 15

Chapter 4 The Limbic System Triggers the Brain Stem:
  Your Reactions..19

Chapter 5 The Neocortex: Your Conscious Mind 25

Understanding the Problem with Your Mind

Chapter 6 So, What's the Problem?..31

Chapter 7 Your Instinctive Brain in Action...............................35

Chapter 8 The Jukebox: Wound Tunes......................................39

Chapter 9 The Instinctive Brain: Your Threat Detector 41

Chapter 10 Insecurities and Self-Esteem 43

Chapter 11 Independence..51

Self-Therapy..53

Understand the Solutions for Your Mind

Chapter 12 The Solution 57

Chapter 13 It's Like Riding a Bicycle 61

Chapter 14 How Healing Happens in Your Brain 65

Chapter 15 Unhealthy Versus Healthy Loops 69

Chapter 16 Managing the Cycle of Emotions...........................73

Healing the Mind 76

Understanding the Mind in Your Relationships

Chapter 17 Four Key Relationships 79

Managing Emotions from your Mind in Daily Life

How You React to Your Emotions During the Day *100*
How to Manage Your Emotions During the Day *101*
Chapter 18 Twelve Take Charge Rhino Tips to Help Manage and
            Change Your Emotions 103
Chapter 19 Summary 121
Chapter 20 Resonate With People 123
Chapter 21 Recognizing Your Spirit 125
Chapter 22 Putting It All Together! 127
Chapter 23 What Is Your Next Step? 133

Appendix

Glossary of Terms 139
Fun Facts about the Ostrich 145
Fun Facts about Rhinos 147
Bibliography 149
About the Author 151
The Rhino Story 155

Preface

What drives you crazy? Is there something that consistently sets you off? Is your mind incapable of shutting off all the chaotic mental chatter and stirring emotions? Why is that? What is the root source of your mind coming up with the things it does? Well, you are about to find out—and discover a great deal more.

This book is designed to give you insights into how the brain is wired and how you can manage your constantly working instinctive brain. *This is your greatest challenge.* A close friend pointed out to me that most people don't want to know how the house is wired—they just want the light to come on when they flip the switch. He may be right. The problem, of course, comes when you flip the switch, and the light *doesn't* come on! Is the problem the bulb? The switch? The circuit breaker? Or, is there no power at all? Who is supposed to fix this? Life has many broken light bulb moments with its petty annoyances, major setbacks, and disappointments. We all have things to overcome. No one comes through unscathed. So, who is going to fix me when my light doesn't come on?

Think about it. No one's life turns out like they thought it would. Have things not worked out quite the way you wanted? When you don't heal your stored pain and disappointments, you live with unhealthy thoughts and emotions, and retain unmet expectations. Coping mechanisms develop and become a way of life. They run in an endless loop in your head and play out in your behaviors and ultimately in your relationships. Track how you handle your relationships to discover the source of the unmet expectations that lower your confidence, harm your relationships, and wreck your happiness.

The brain processes an incredible amount of information before you are consciously aware. That can be a challenging thought, if not downright overwhelming—at least, until you know how to think clearly and make good decisions. Soon you will know so much more. The result is healthy thinking, genuine peace, better relationships, and comfort in the knowledge that you will be okay.

When you learn and apply these principles, you will believe more in *yourself.* You are wired to succeed! It truly is all about what happens between the ears.

Welcome to the discovery of the *instinctive brain,* the *conscious mind,* and the *human spirit.*

Illustrations are used to provide a visual of the concepts and principles. Insights and success stories are in italics to help you apply the concepts in real life.

Knowledge fosters a healthy mind.

A healthy mind fosters healthy relationships.

Healthy relationships foster a healthy society.

Introduction

~ ~ ~

Anytime you make a positive difference in someone's life, it is rewarding.

~ ~ ~

With your permission . . .

Let's start with yours!

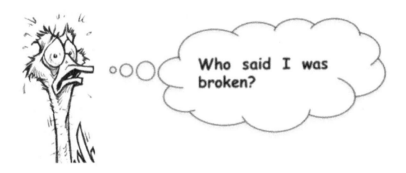

We are all, every one of us, abnormal—meaning no one comes through life unscathed.

Oh, really? Who says? Truth be told, we all do. We all, at some point, feel insecure, unworthy, or insufficient. We all feel that something about us isn't okay. Now, enough of that, let's get you a healthier perspective—one that will free you like never before.

Why Renew Your Mind?

Because you get results! Peace. Healthy relationships. Success. That's why.

To get those results, we need to understand how the brain functions:

- **Your *instinctive brain* is a computer.** (It's not a person; it doesn't have a will. Stop acting like there's another person in your head with authority over you—there is not.)
- **Your *personality* is the software to your computer.** (Your personality is not who you are; it's just a starting point. Your decisions determine who you are).
- **Your *experiences* are the data that your software uses.**
- **You—your heart and spirit—are separate from these three.**
- **Using your conscious mind, you are designed to manage and override much of what your instinctive brain feeds you.**

You weren't born with all the stresses that your instinctive brain thrives on. You acquired them from the bumps and bruises you got along the way. I call these whale scars. When you see a whale, you can't help but notice the scars. The whale has overcome threats and challenges to live and become a mature, beautiful creature, but not without battle scars. Your whale scars come from your life experiences and are stored deep in your memory, not on the surface of your skin. These old scars can mislead your emotional expectations in life. Some need to be corrected or healed. Left uncorrected over time, they evolve from being coping mechanisms that once served you well into unhealthy behaviors that do not serve you today. You may be blind to their effects. In fact, your brain will tend to block you from dealing with them as part of its intent to protect you. These scars will continue to affect your decisions and your relationships until you address them. However, you were created to be whole and healthy when you were born, before the whale scars appeared.

The healthy original you is still alive and wants to come out and play, but your brain has recorded these whale scars and applies them daily to your emotions, distorting your perceptions and limiting your potential. That potential is your peace, your success, and healthy relationships. That potential is yours to choose and experience. You just need to know how.

Without even knowing it, most people judge their lives by their scars, not by their true healthy self. Do not measure yourself by your scars or imperfections. If you didn't have your scars, how would you view yourself? Think about that for a minute. You can manage and heal any unhealthy emotions etched into your whale scars. You can see yourself as a whole, healthy person and get on with *living,* not merely existing. In addition, here's something magical that happens as a sort of bonus: When you change you, others change, too! They see you differently and have to respond differently. And you gain new confidence.

Everyone has something to overcome; this is why abnormal is normal. The real problem is how your brain reflects on past events and how you manage those thoughts coming from your brain. *Managing thoughts changes emotions.* This means you can free yourself by taking charge of your perspective. The real beauty is that you have much more of yourself yet to discover and experience!

You will be introduced to insights and methods to help you think healthy and helpful thoughts instead of overreacting from your emotions. You may be surprised at how much overreacting you do. The cartoon illustrations show you how the mind works in different situations. The goal is to learn how you can have control over your emotional and mental traps.

This book is not meant to replace the benefits psychology and counseling provide, but rather to present a practical, sometimes humorous way to find a healthy perspective amid the hurly-burly of daily life. You can think better and more efficiently when you apply these insights. Putting these insights into your life may enhance the benefits of any professional help you seek. You are wired to overcome and designed to succeed. You just didn't know how before. Here you will learn shortcuts to simplify the process and make it easy to put into practice. Gain success in one area and you will quickly be able to apply this strategy to other areas.

With all the complexities of being human (body, mind, spirit, emotion, experiences, genetics, and environment), success still often boils down to one thing. This short passage of dialogue in the movie *City Slickers,* between Jack Palance as Curly and Billy Crystal as Mitch, expresses it aptly:

Curly: Do you know what the secret of life is?
Mitch: No, what?
Curly: This. [Holds up one finger]
Mitch: Your finger?
Curly: One thing. Just one thing. You stick to that and everything else don't … mean . . .
Mitch: That's great, but what's the one thing?
Curly: That's what you've got to figure out. [Mitch looks at his finger.]

I love that last line, because it is so true for each of us. People become locked into a childhood emotional wound, an unmet expectation, or a poor self-perception. We are blind to these filters, yet we each have to face them because only then can our healthy life begin. Until we figure out that one thing, we are just coping. My coaching helps people find and unravel the perception that is blocking their potential and then guides them to discover and finally live their true desires. After all, everyone grows tired of experiencing what they *don't* want.

Even on your best day of striving for that true desire, your instinctive brain is locked on an experience from long ago that is constantly derailing you. You are the only one who can free you from your instinctive brain. No one can do it for you. The key is to know what the issue is and how to resolve it. Often, once you discover it, it's as clear as looking at yourself in a mirror. Changing the lens that you see yourself through and catching years of thoughts and behaviors is the key. Healing painful emotions can be an enjoyable experience. It doesn't have to hurt.

Fear need not be part of this process, but overcoming presumed fear might be. Fears are healthy when there is real danger, but some fears are myths—perceptions or beliefs that don't reflect reality. Instead of fear, a healthier perception will give you peace.

This work is a process, and each step dovetails with the others. The first step is to understand how the brain and mind work together, both instinctively and consciously. These two parts operate independently from each other, but they are also engineered to work together. Your instinctive brain will *challenge you (with Alerts!),* but will also *follow* your conscious mind. Knowing this gives you permission to use logic to manage your emotions. Do you find this a little confusing? Don't worry, it will soon become clear to you.

In this book, you will learn:

1. how your brain is structured and generates thoughts and emotions;
2. how your relationships are affected as a result, and;
3. what you *can do* to override reactionary tendencies and instead maintain peace and confidence, improve relationships, and calm unsettled emotions.

You are invited and encouraged to complete all five steps. Once you do you will never look at life the same way again!

Remember that there isn't another person in your head with the authority to make you respond or behave a certain way. Stop acting like there is. When you decide to change your patterns, the brain will do its job.

A Five-Step Journey to Renew Your Mind

1. Discover how your brain works: Reading *Managing Your Crazy Self!* is the first step. We will explore how to redirect and control your thoughts and emotions. It's all about you.

The next four steps are presented in the Five Steps to Renew Your Mind workshop, which includes training, assessments, books, workbook, and personal coaching. Learn more at www.cerosinc.com.

2. Learn how your personality is hardwired: Complete assessments to determine behavior style, motivators, love language (how you feel affirmed), learning style, emotional intelligence, and gifts. Then review *Managing Your Crazy Self Personality Dynamics* with Randy. Your personality is not who you are, it's just your unique starting point, and the way your brain filters thoughts and emotions. You can override your unhealthy tendencies.

3. Understand how your experiences feed and trigger your instinctive brain: Discover where you have been, where you are today, and where you want to go using the *Managing Your Crazy Self Workbook*. Find out where your thoughts and emotions (including emotional wounds) come from. Learn how to optimize your thinking. Set and achieve short- and long-range goals. Experience a more productive, peaceful mind and new successes. It's all about correcting old data that your instinctive brain is using to trigger your emotions and perspectives so that you can experience more joy.

4. Gain insights and direction from personal coaching: Coaching is an expertise that helps you navigate to success quickly, using customized shortcuts to achieve maximum results with minimal effort. You'll receive feedback and encouragement to keep you moving in the right direction, so you don't stall out or fall back into old habits. You can't see what the coach sees. It's about moving forward efficiently, using constructive tips and insights without all the emotional drama.

5. Enjoy the full YOU! *Your spirit is calling to connect with you, but your instinctive brain is in the way.* Discover how to connect better with your spirit and enjoy real fulfillment in life. It's about putting all of you together and stepping into the life you were meant to live.

Note: Visit www.cerosinc.com for videos, seminars, and coaching that will help you better understand and apply these concepts to your life. It may also be helpful to refer periodically to the glossary of terms in the Appendix.

Understanding the

Structure of Your Mind

This is where your crazy starts!

Chapter 1

Meet the Ostrich and the Rhino

For simplicity's sake, we can think of your brain as having two parts: an *instinctive brain* (reactive) and a *conscious mind* (intentional).

The Ostrich
Instinctive Brain
"Reactive"
(Crazy Self)

The Rhino
Conscious Mind
"Intentional"
(Healthy You)

Once you understand how the thoughts and emotions flow in each part of your brain, you can manage how they affect your behaviors and relationships. Your conscious mind is *supposed* to override your instinctive brain. That's how the brain is wired.

Not all thoughts come from the same part of your brain. Imagine that a driver cuts you off in traffic, almost sending you into the ditch. You flare up with anger as your instinctive brain thinks, "That driver is an idiot!" But another thought is also happening as your conscious mind thinks, "I'm going to avoid that car."

You can go back and forth quickly between these two, but you can't be in both parts of the brain at same time. Every minute of every day, your thoughts flow back and forth. If you listen to the wrong one, then you are nurturing your crazy self.

DEFINITIONS

crazy[1] [**krey**-zee]

Adjective
1. senseless; impractical; shaky; lacking discretion
2. intensely emotional; extreme unease

Synonyms
imprudent, irrational, illogical, totally unsound (inaccurate, unhealthy), unstable

Antonyms
sane, calm, stable, strong, healthy

managing[2] [**man**-ij-eng]

Verb
1. to bring about or succeed in accomplishing, sometimes despite difficulty or hardship
2. to take charge or authority; to care for

Synonyms
arrange, guide, regulate, take care of, handle

Antonyms
neglect, ignore, bumble

---

[1] Definitions, synonyms, and antonyms adapted from dictionary.com and yourdictionary.com.
[2] Definitions, synonyms, and antonyms adapted from dictionary.com, oxforddictionaries.com and thesaurus.com.

Chapter 2

The Physical Structure of Your Brain:

A Blueprint

Why are these two characters of the brain important to you?
Because your thoughts bounce back and forth between them all
day. Not knowing how to manage this can drive you crazy! Each
part of your brain is designed for a specific purpose and generates
different thoughts and emotions to help you function in different
settings.

Logic and Reason   **Reactions**
Big Brain   Pea Brain

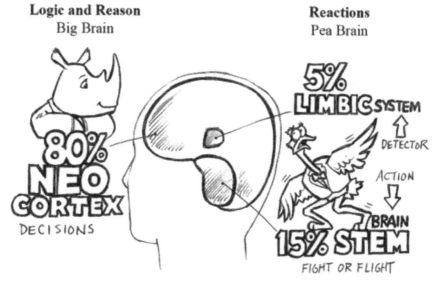

All information must pass through the limbic system's detector to be scanned for potential danger.

The conscious mind (the rhino) represents the larger part of your
brain and is called the *neocortex.* The instinctive brain (the ostrich)
is made up of two smaller areas called the *limbic system* and the
brain stem. The *limbic system,* which I call the pea brain, is a small

13

area in the center of the brain, and the brain stem (often called the lizard brain) is located in the lower back part of the brain.

The pea brain thinks, Oh, no! There's the boss. I feel intimidated! But most bosses don't want intimidated employees. They want confident thinkers and doers. Instead, use the bigger part of your brain (the neocortex) to say good to see you, boss."

Here's the bottom line: pea brain thinking doesn't let you achieve anything close to your true potential!

Chapter 3

The Instinctive Brain Begins
with the Limbic System

Every thought and emotion begins in the instinctive limbic system (your security system) or is rerouted there to be scanned for potential danger. So, you can imagine that a lot happens in your instinctive brain before your conscious mind (big brain) engages a decent thought.

The limbic system works like a computer security system. It scans incoming data looking for danger and sends Alerts!

Anytime something sets you off, that is your instinctive alert system in action. For example, you startle when you hear a door slam. When someone raises his or her voice at you, you suddenly feel defensive. Or you're annoyed to discover, too late, that there is no toilet paper in the bathroom. Remember when you jerked your hand away after touching something hot? You tend to react before you reason.

From here on remember: *The limbic system is not trying to drive you crazy.* It's just trying to protect you from danger. It is your instinctive, protective brain at work.

Limbic System Traits

The limbic system does a fine job of managing your body's organs and involuntary processes including your heartbeat, respiration, sleep, digestion, and healing. In other words, the physiological things you don't have to think about are taken care of thanks to the limbic system.

The limbic system also serves as your database. It records every experience and emotion in your life, both good and bad. It is important to understand that the limbic system is *not* wired to *initiate* good thoughts—just to send warnings to protect you. *Good* thoughts are recorded in the limbic system, but they are only initiated from the conscious mind (neocortex) when you choose them.

Your instinctive brain is your security system, continuously scanning every second of every day, for any possible danger. It evaluates your present with memories from your past. It never shuts off. This is a good thing, because you need your brain to protect you. However, because it runs continuously, you have to *manage* it continuously. You have to use your conscious mind to correct the instinctive brain's warnings. You do not need to react to the constant millisecond scanning of weather updates, emails, phone calls, to-do items, fears, etc. Your instinctive brain cannot manage all that stress. If you don't use your conscious mind to manage your unconscious brain, you will exhaust your energy and create unhealthy coping mechanisms. Others will also be affected, just as you are affected by someone else's coping mechanisms.

The limbic system creates and thrives on insecurities (unresolved emotional wounds or unmet expectations). These insecurities become key to your Alert! protection system. They are formed in your instinctive brain, usually when you are a child before your conscious mind has matured. Your instinctive brain, on the other hand, has been cranking along full throttle since birth, recording every action and emotion and sending Alerts!

Another important fact you need to be aware of is that your instinctive mind does NOT comprehend time. The instinctive brain thinks any unresolved past perception or wound is still happening right now, and it continues thinking so until you resolve it. That is why memories of past events can stir up feelings just as if they were happening right now. In other words, much of what you tend to feel now came from long ago. This is one area where the brain can mislead you. The good news is that you don't have to be stuck living with emotions from your past. Your brain is wired so that you can resolve these perceptions, thereby healing the associated wounds. Corrections override the Alerts! They reduce your fears, give you peace, and make way for a new confidence. You alone can make these corrections; no one can do it for you. You learn how to do it, just like you learned to feed yourself, dress yourself, and make your own decisions. Sometimes all you need is a subtle insight to give you the ability. However, that insight is incredibly powerful.

Be aware that the limbic system does NOT manage your daily activities or relationships well at all. That's not what it was made to do. You are to manage your calendar and relationships with your conscious mind. Many problems that surface in relationships are due to your reactions to Alerts! that come from your past. This is often why emotional arguments happen. Your reactions trigger the other person's reactions, and soon neither of you knows why the discussion became such a big mess. You are both upset and in a reactionary discussion. The point is your Alerts! originated from an unmet expectation of a past relationship, and they will affect your current relationships until they are corrected. When you identify and resolve the origin of the Alert! it is freeing.

Often I have found simple humor (not humor that criticizes) can be used to bypass the brain's usual Alert! reactions and help provide a resolution. Humor can help us hear and accept wonderful truths. Humor switches *where you are thinking* in your head. It buys you a little time and changes your emotions. Using humor can be as simple as saying something like, "This isn't exactly going the way I was hoping." Humor is only one of the methods you can use to move from the instinctive brain to your conscious mind. Learn not to react—that is the trap to avoid.

The good news is that the protection your instinctive mind provides you has helped you stay alive up to today. However, healing is better. The limbic system is all about surviving by avoiding problems. It thrives by sensing fear and using emotions to maintain protection. These fears, however, can impede confidence, trust, and other strengths you should enjoy. If you didn't remember your fears, you would forget to look both ways before chasing a ball across the street. The fear helps keep you from getting hit by a car. The key is knowing when to override your fears and acting consciously.

Your instinctive brain cannot help you move forward. It can only help you survive. The conscious mind is what helps you move forward. Use each part of your brain for the right purpose. You wouldn't rely on your hand to do your breathing or your foot to do your hearing, would you? Also, your instinctive brain DOES NOT TRUST. It scans. If no threat is identified it passes on information to the conscious mind. But it doesn't really trust. It can't trust any more than your computer can trust you.

Chapter 4

The Limbic System Triggers the Brain Stem: Your Reactions

When the limbic system perceives danger, it triggers the brain stem to initiate a fight, flight, or freeze reaction. Remember, these reactions are not the real you, they are just your instinctive responses.

Fight!   Flight!   Freeze!

The brain stem operates to keep you alive by reacting either with fight, flight, or freeze. Picture an animal in the wild, on high alert, ready to run to avoid trouble, or to charge and attack, or freezing like a deer in the headlights. Once you are in fight, flight, or freeze response, there are no other options. Your instinctive brain is doing its job of protecting you by staying in this mode until the perceived danger is gone.

Imagine how many conversations people have had that were just fight, flight, or freeze reactions. They weren't having a healthy conversation at all! The solution is to capture and embrace your Alert! reactions and redirect them. Think to yourself, be aware, but don't get sucked in.

Fight behaviors can include arguing, disobeying, acting out (making mischief), or physical actions such as slamming doors, hitting, yelling, and so on. These behaviors are different in character and origin than those that result from confronting challenges in a healthy way using the conscious mind.

Flight behaviors may include withdrawal, avoidance, silence, feeling subdued, passive-aggressive actions, depression, or feeling victimized or defeated.

Freeze behavior occurs when you don't know what to do because you don't see a way to fight back or run for protection. Freeze is a numbed sensation, when you feel you can't think or move. You are stunned; you don't fight, and you don't withdraw. You just freeze in disbelief or an inability to take any action. This reaction can become an *emotional freeze point* that will affect you repeatedly.

A freeze response may result from the death of a loved one, a divorce, or from an everyday experience that had quite an effect on you, kind of like hitting your funny bone but in an emotional way. Freeze points can be serious and need to be expertly addressed to resolve them because they don't go away by themselves. When your emotions become frozen in reaction to a life event they will not allow you to connect fully with your feelings in that area until the issue is resolved. Freeze points can be healed, but you have to deal with them with a healthy resolve. It can be like massaging a physical injury; it may hurt at first, but stimulation can help it to heal.

You can default to fight, flight, or freeze any time emotions are triggered and connect with your instinctive brain. Don't fear these instinctive reactions, they are just Alert! signals. Be ready to snap out of it by using your thoughts to switch to productive conscious thinking instead. This requires a thought or action to interrupt the pattern. Different methods work for different people. Some prefer humor, some focus on a positive thought, and others take physical action like going for a walk or exercising. Whatever you choose, make it nonreactive and productive. If you can combine two or more methods, the results will be quicker and more effective. For example, listen to an upbeat song and dance to the music. Write a thank you note with a humorous thought to someone you appreciate. It can be helpful to get advice from someone you think would handle the situation better than you. Tell yourself it is okay to address what freezes you.

 When you sense Alerts! your brain releases chemicals and hormones such as adrenaline throughout the body to prepare you for action.[3] When it's happening, you can feel the tension in your muscles and sense the hair rising on your neck. You probably know people who are wired to overreact, whose brain stems keep their fearful emotions running high. Over time, this tendency can lock them into fear and anxiety and lead to obsessive or addictive habits. If this is your pattern and you want to move towards emotional health, you need to learn to calm yourself and recognize that you are safe and will be okay.

The brain stem doesn't reason or weigh positive alternatives; it just reacts. Your Alert! reactions will surface repeatedly until you resolve them. Staying in fight, flight, or freeze thinking creates unneeded stress and takes a toll on performance, relationships, and overall well being. So, don't fear addressing your Alert! reactions. Notice your behaviors. Identify them. Ask others to validate your perceptions. Then determine and implement healthy alternative actions. This process requires *you to be vulnerable at first,* but the benefits are tremendously freeing.

Another reason to address fight, flight, or freeze reactions is that long-term stress tends to find a physical outlet and will most likely surface in a weak part of your body. Stress can lead to all kinds of ailments including acne, shingles, skin cancer, digestion difficulties, high blood pressure, joint and muscle issues, organ

---

[3] Bill Crawford, PhD, *Life from the Top of the Mind* (Houston: Florence Publishing, 2006), 72.

dysfunction, and sleep problems (including teeth grinding). The chemicals your body releases to prepare you for fight, flight, or freeze can harm you over time if you experience Alert! reactions day in and day out.

On the other hand, healthy stress and productive thoughts produce chemicals that can reduce pain and ailments and create better health. Medicine has its place, but it often treats the symptoms, not the cause. Reducing unhealthy stress reduces the need for medicines. Often, people go for years not realizing that the source of their poor health is their unhealthy thinking. The good news is that healthy thinking can start anytime. Your body replaces every cell over seven years, so if you start now, your body will reap the benefits of low- or at least lower-stress living. So, whatever stress you have in your life, be it divorce, addictions, job loss, health issues, or just having teenagers, your body is wired to renew its cells.

One quick, simple way to reduce stress in the moment is to take long, slow breaths through your nose. This triggers healthy chemicals from your brain, whereas shallow, panting breaths through the mouth trigger anxiety and the release of unhealthy chemicals. Practice releasing stress throughout each day. Incorporate quick breaks, exercise, hobbies, giving back to your community, and so on to give your mind balance and break up stressful thought patterns. Do not hold stress in without some healthy release.

Once when I was giving blood, the nurse took my blood pressure and it was crazy high! She told me to go sit in a room for twenty minutes and be in my happy place. I thought of relaxing in the outdoors on a spring day. She took my blood pressure again, and it was 120/80—well within the healthy range. My body wasn't unhealthy; my thinking was. It is worth taking a moment periodically throughout your day to reboot to healthy thinking. Your body will thank you.

All thoughts start, or are routed, through the limbic system for scanning. Any danger perceived is immediately routed to the brain stem and sending your mind into full protection mode. Only when there is no danger, or the danger is gone, will thoughts move to the conscious mind. You don't realize how fast this scanning happens or even that it is happening when no danger is flagged. However, when you sense danger you know it. You feel it. When you feel danger, you then have to determine if it is real or just a reaction.

Tip: If you are not going to die, let the emotion go.

As a rule of thumb, if you feel your emotional reactions kicking in, stop and ask yourself, am I going to die? If not, let it go. In other words, let go of your emotionally wounded thinking. Think conscious thoughts instead. The most dangerous thing most of us do is drive a car (unless you work in law enforcement or the military). You aren't likely to die in most situations of life, so why get so worried or upset? You are reinforcing wounded thinking and behaviors that don't serve you well.

Learn to identify which reaction you default to: fight, flight, or freeze. Once you recognize your go-to reaction, you can choose a healthier response. You may default to different reactions in different situations. You may argue with authority and freeze with rejection. Don't fear becoming aware of your reactions. Write them down and track them. Think about what you do and how you feel in different situations, especially when you feel hurt or have a weakness. You can find a solution and start to practice making healthy choices instead. Once you experience this new success you will begin to trust yourself to face other issues in your life.

You've met the ostrich that represents your instinctive brain. Now let's meet the other character in your head—the rhino, which represents your conscious mind.

Chapter 5

The Neocortex: Your Conscious Mind

Your conscious mind is where you make choices and where you can thrive. You become the decisions you make.

This is you!

A new and better you continues to evolve as you learn.
It's happening all day, every day.

Trust, innovation, creativity, and confidence do not exist in the limbic system. To have these experiences in your life, you have to move your thoughts to the conscious mind, which I call the rhino mind. You don't want to be stuck with your reactions to your ostrich's instinctive thinking! Take charge of every thought. Discover the untapped you!

Conscious Mind Traits

Your conscious mind is the REAL YOU. Conscious decisions happen *only* in the neocortex, where you experience purposeful reasoning. Your rhino mind is where you choose to generate positive feelings and experiences and heal old emotional scars. Each new accomplishment or healthy experience gives you new knowledge and trust. This is why success breeds success. Your memory has those experiences to draw upon.

You are not just your personality, nor are you just your experiences. Too many people say that's just the way I am. What happens to you doesn't define you. What you do about it defines you. You are always *becoming you* as you grow in knowledge and experience. Your brain is big so that you have room to grow, and it is always ready to create. Use all of it. You have a wonderful upside, as you will see.

You are the only one with the control and authority to manage your thoughts. To function with healthy thoughts and emotions, you have to override the instinctive brain. Don't fear this; embrace it. Practice and master it.

By choosing to think from your conscious mind rather than merely reacting from your instinctive brain, you generate healthy chemicals in your system instead of unhealthy chemicals associated with the fight, flight, or freeze response from your limbic system. You get to choose your thinking, and your brain automatically sends the chemicals.

As you experience new successes, you will gain a new confidence and the belief that you can master a healthier you. This healthier you creates more good memories to draw from, which builds trust in yourself. Would your life be better if you made those choices instead of remaining stuck in reaction mode? You bet it would!

You choose which part of the brain you inhabit—and, therefore, what emotions and chemicals are released into your body. You are the source of how you feel.

Unhealthy example: I am so upset; I can't even watch the game today.

Healthy example: I am upset, but tonight is football night. I'll deal with it tomorrow. Tonight I am going to enjoy the game!

Understanding the

Problem with Your Mind

Reacting isn't your only option.

Chapter 6

So, What's the Problem?

Picture a mature instinctive brain and an immature
conscious mind talking.

Wow Ostrich, calm down.

Your instinctive brain (ostrich) is essentially mature at birth. Your
conscious mind (rhino) does not mature until years later.

Years of early experiences and unmet expectations are
stored in your memory banks long before you can use reason.
These unmet emotional expectations are created and stored as your
benchmark for all future experiences by your instinctive brain.
These benchmarks stay alive in your memory and unconsciously

distort your perceptions throughout your life until you resolve them.

In the womb, you are not aware of the universe. All of your needs are met. Once you are born you experience being cold, hungry, wet, wanting to be held, and so on. You interact with the outside world and your caregivers. Your instinctive brain is working pretty much at full maturity right off the bat, recording every event, sensing danger, and sending Alerts! Its job is to Alert! and protect you, to keep you safe. Your conscious mind doesn't know what to do yet. So, you observe, explore, and learn to navigate your environment all through your early years. Eventually, you learn to say "no!" and "mine!" These are powerful words in a child's early development.

In contrast, your conscious mind takes years to develop fully. You don't know how to eat, dress, go to the bathroom, or make responsible decisions. During these years, your instinctive brain is recording countless expectations, some of which will need a corrective override. Some expectations experienced before your conscious mind matured are not applicable now. However, your instinctive brain doesn't know that. It is doing its job recording and scanning full throttle. Your conscious mind is focused on exploring the present, not correcting what happened in the past. Even if you knew something needed correcting, you likely wouldn't know how to do it. So, the past keeps playing in the background of your instinctive brain and triggering reactions until it is corrected. An interesting question to ponder is why some wounds sear into our memory and others do not influence us at all.

Somewhere along the way you expected love, acceptance, and care from a caregiver or a relationship that you didn't receive, at least not in the way you expected. It could be a simple perception of not getting what you thought you should, or perhaps someone actively harmed you. Somewhere an expectation wasn't met and that experience was etched in your instinctive brain. That experience became a baseline expectation from then on and plays out today and every day as if it was happening right now. This is your instinctive brain working hard to protect you, not trying to make you feel bad or guilty.

Sometimes a single event can shape your perceptions for the rest of your life in a way that isn't helpful. Remember, the instinctive brain is programmed to protect you from danger. As you mature, you are to correct unhelpful perceptions. You didn't know how to deal with it at the time because your conscious mind wasn't mature enough. Memories play unconsciously all day, every day, in your brain as if they are still happening right now, until you resolve them.

Did you get that? *Problems in the instinctive brain are waiting to be resolved by the conscious mind.* They don't have to permanently scar you. Emotional reactions to problems are signals. They identify an opportunity to address something in you that needs to be dealt with. Until you deal with them, reactionary coping skills help you survive in the short-term, but aren't necessarily healthy behaviors. Some of us are not aware all this is going on in our head. Watch your behaviors and ask why you react that way. You can resolve and heal your deep, unmet expectations and change the old emotions and perceptions to healthy ones. No one can do it for you. You are under no obligation to hold on to deep-seated emotional reactions that cause you (and others you interact with) pain. Make one simple change and see what a difference it will make.

If you are like most people, you greatly underestimate the effect the first old wound has on you today. It formed a powerful baseline of expectations you use to assess all future situations. Though it was formed when you were young to protect you, this subconscious filter will not bring you any satisfaction today. If not corrected, your instinctive brain will only mislead you by surfacing your old issues over and over. Today's emotions are being driven by past perceptions formed when your conscious mind wasn't mature. Your Alert! system is working from that unmet emotional need from the past, and it needs correction or healing for you to be healthy today. You may not think you have a wound like this, but the odds are you do.

Interestingly, you don't have to have a bad childhood to need to heal a wound from an unmet emotional need. You could have had a great childhood. The instinctive brain records and evaluates everything, even before the conscious mind is able to reason. Imagine, for example, that your mother told you that you were special, or that you could be great. Bing! The thought gets seared into your mind that you are to be something special. From then on, you wonder, what is special about me? Who will tell me? When will I find out? Your mother meant to encourage you, but your instinctive brain interpreted her words very differently, maybe even as something you felt pressure to live up to.

On the other hand, your wound could have formed from a natural need. Perhaps your father didn't show love or acceptance, or your individuality was disapproved of rather than encouraged. All of these situations create a longing for something you expected that didn't materialize. In all likelihood, your parent wasn't trying to hurt you. In fact, they were very likely trying to resolve unmet emotional needs from their own childhood.

Old emotions and fears play constantly in your instinctive brain and can easily trap you unless you take charge of them. You are supposed to eventually learn to heal them, not just deal with them. Healing is also part of your brain's design. However, healing requires your willingness to tackle the issue, and that you be willing to override strong emotions. These emotions feel so real, but they are just perceptions. I call mine myths because I know they aren't permanent and I have chosen not to be afraid of them. They are waiting for me to take charge of them and to grow from them. Just like you crawl before you walk, healing these old emotions and fears is a development that is meant to happen.

Get ready for a great new discovery of you. Now that is mature rhino thinking!

Chapter 7

Your Instinctive Brain in Action

This is what your instinctive brain might look like if you could see it in action.

Careful! Oh, no! Not again! Run! Defend! Attack! Freeze!

What wounded worry signs would be on your brain's bulletin board?

The Problem with Instinctive Brain Traits

The painful event is long over, but the emotions are still alive, and they will stay alive until you change your perspective about the event. You weren't born with your instinctive brain's fears. The problem came from an experience along the way (again, those pesky whale scars). Your reaction is unconsciously reflecting past pain, but you don't have to let it represent who you are today. Don't let it trap you. That reaction comes from an event in the past. Not redirecting your past emotions to the conscious mind in the present, well, *that* is the problem. Become conscious of your reactions.

You don't panic at every severe weather alert. You look to see if it applies to you, and then plan accordingly. If you aren't in danger of dying, then you don't overreact. Apply that strategy to every Alert! your brain sends you. If you aren't going to die, let it go. You now know that these Alerts! are coming in constantly. Therefore, you must manage them constantly.

Stay out of fight, flight, or freeze thinking. Reactionary thinking causes the instinctive brain to trigger repeatedly, sending you Alerts! and leading you to fight, flight, or freeze thinking and behaviors. This hooks you into unhealthy coping mechanisms and poor habits. Reactionary thinking is a lot like having your own social media wired to your brain and blasting you with endless junk mail and spam (unnecessary information and emotions).

Learn new ways to think and create a healthy response. Later you will see examples of how to make those changes.

To keep emotional Alerts! from your instinctive brain from trapping you, pause and reboot your thoughts often during your day. Plan every few hours, or after a stressful moment, to listen to a song, think a wonderful thought, talk with a friend, or whatever works for you to reboot.

Here's why great ball teams are consistent winners: They believe they are winners. They may have lost the last game, but they let it go and move on. They don't fear losing; they focus on winning. Their winning percentage may be just a few points better than most teams, but it makes all the difference in winning the division. You have to choose to believe something until you know it from experience. This ability to choose is what overrides your protective instinctive brain's emotional signals.

Great batters don't hope they are going to get a hit; they believe they will. They don't sweat over the last strikeout. That play is over. They hit balls that aren't in the strike zone; they often swing and miss. They swing believing they will hit the ball, not fretting that they won't. They still strike out more often than they get a hit. A great hitter bats a .300 average—that means he is not hitting the ball 70 percent of the time. Is he a winner? You better believe it! Choose thoughts and beliefs that are good for you.

You will win every day when you reboot and keep emotional Alerts! from shaking your focus. Let's look at some analogies of the instinctive brain in action.

Chapter 8

The Jukebox: Wound Tunes

Your unmet emotions are stored in your memory and play like songs in a jukebox.

SAME OLD SONGS

Childhood wound tunes play continually in the instinctive brain.

Your instinctive brain is like a jukebox playing old records of your wounded memories. We might call these wound tunes. This jukebox plays all your old heartache songs, and twists the words to fit the unmet expectations. Your ostrich will sing your songs passionately, and you feel them deeply so you think they are true.

Here's the thing: The jukebox can only play the tunes on its playlist. Your brain only plays the memories it recorded. If you want to hear a good song, you've got to put it on by creating a new experience and memory you want to live by. New songs help heal old wound tunes.

Chapter 9

The Instinctive Brain: Your Threat Detector

A metal detector doesn't know the difference between a gun and a belt buckle; neither does your brain.

Thus, your conscious mind must constantly override your brain's false Alerts!

An airport metal detector is another apt analogy for how the instinctive brain functions. The metal detector looks for a weapon made of metal, like a gun or knife. The problem is that the metal detector doesn't know the difference between a gun and a belt buckle—it just detects metal and sounds the same Alert! for either one. Your brain does essentially the same thing with your emotions; it triggers reactions to false Alerts! as well as real Alerts! Your conscious mind has to tell the difference and override the false Alerts! Not making this distinction will drive you crazy!

At one airport, my son went through security and was flagged by the alarm. The security agent scanned him with a wand and found a tiny foil gum wrapper wadded into a ball in his pocket.

The agent explained that the scanner was set on high sensitivity. The agent let him go, of course, but it was unnerving. If your scanner is set to be too sensitive, you set yourself up for unnecessary issues and delays. You can learn to reboot to non-Alert! status quickly.

Any perception of danger sends an Alert! as neurons send information to the brain stem. This happens very, very fast. Most Alerts! are not about anything that can hurt us today—just warnings about wounded emotions from the past. These Alerts! can happen often in your day.

Not only does the airport metal detector sound false Alerts! it doesn't have the wiring to compliment you. You'll never hear it say, "Great hair!" or "Love your shoes!" So, don't expect it. Just as you have to put the songs you want to hear on your jukebox, you have to choose complimentary thoughts about yourself.

Although happy memories are also stored in the instinctive brain, they are called up through the conscious mind by using one of your five senses: sight, sound, touch, smell, or taste. If you smell a fresh cake baking, you will think, mmm, I like cake. That thought is coming from your conscious mind in response to the scent, not from your instinctive brain. So, do not expect your instinctive brain to encourage you with happy memories and thoughts. Learn to choose to think calm, energizing thoughts to redirect your brain from Alerts!

Learn to catch your behaviors when you react in unhealthy ways. If someone compliments you, you may deny it because your instinctive brain discredits what you heard. For instance, someone may say, "You look terrific!" If you reply, "Ugh, I couldn't get my hair to do right," that is your instinctive brain discrediting the compliment. Instead, use your conscious mind to choose to say, "Thank you!" And then choose to think, 'Wow, I look great today!"

Realize that you won't naturally wake up and say to yourself, I look marvelous! You have to choose to like the person in the mirror, without indulging in self-criticism.

Chapter 10

Insecurities and Self-Esteem

Insecurities are formed and stored from old perceptions. While you consciously pursue successes, your instinctive mind Alerts! you of your insecurities.

The instinctive brain says, "I am unsure, I wish I could find my confidence (trust, self-esteem, self-worth, etc.)!"

The conscious mind says, "Hey, I'm right here!"

Your instinctive brain is waiting for *you* to act with confidence. Choose it!

The instinctive brain and its insecurities *will not* ask for help from the conscious mind, even though it is just inches away. It can only send Alerts! Insecurities from old wounds can sabotage your confidence and success, and will ultimately affect your relationships. You, using your conscious mind, must decide to move forward. The instinctive brain will comply and immediately seek the next Alert! it finds. This is how the brain works. Thoughts lead to Alerts! You either react or override the Alert! Repeat. All day, every day. The more calmly you learn to think the less you react.

Insecurities are Rooted in Your Lost Self

When you are born, your instinctive brain doesn't know what danger is yet. Your brain is set to record that first unwanted experience to protect you from future danger. But it doesn't know what that danger will be until you live it. Once you experience the first deep unmet expectation, it becomes stored as an emotional wound. It becomes a baseline insecurity against which all your future experiences will be measured. All other fears are based on the first one. Take the time to think of your first fear. When you can reframe it with new understanding, your brain will apply that to subsequent fears as well.

Fears feel real even when you know there is no actual danger. I used to see the shadow of my tall clothes rack with its curved wooden hooks in my room at night. In the daylight, it was just a wooden clothes rack. At night, the shadows of the hooks became scary claws. I knew they weren't claws, but I was still scared. Fortunately, I was able to override that fear. Looking back at it with some humor, I thought, the clothes rack never attacked me; maybe it was afraid of me, too!

Learning to reframe your fears will take practice, but your fears will become less intense and less frequent over time. It is a simple formula. Unmet expectations from childhood experiences are stored in your memory and used by your brain to affect how you feel in a given situation today. You can override the wound from the old perception with new understanding to form a new perception. Doing so is freeing; it heals you. You don't have to change the past event, just the perception of the event. Find a new way to look at it. Then you are free to explore life using your potential again. It has been said that we are most brilliant at three years old because we don't yet realize any consequences. After that, we let consequences diminish our brilliance.

Your unmet emotional expectations most likely came from an interaction in a relationship. Either there was something someone said, never said, did, or didn't do. Because a critical unmet expectation initiated from a relationship those emotions will resurface in the context of future relationships. Most often, you are not conscious this is happening. Therapist and author Harville Hendrix calls our response to this kind of wounding the "the lost self."[4]

Your most critical unmet expectation creates a deep want or need that becomes an insecurity. You most likely do not recognize the importance of that specific event's effect, though you react to it continuously. Therefore, it becomes part of what Hendrix calls the lost self. Lost because you don't usually recall what the original wound was, or know what to do about it. Your brain tends to mask or block it, which is a protection in itself. For example, you worked hard to please your mom and never felt validated, so you are too strict or too permissive with your kids today. Your bike was stolen so now you keep things forever; or perhaps you were abused by a stranger so you are afraid to go to new places. Your hidden insecurity will affect your current

---

[4] Harville Hendrix, PhD, *Getting the Love You Want: A Guide for Couples,* 20th anniversary edition (New York: St. Martin's Press, 2008), 24.

behaviors, whether you repeat the old pattern or react with the opposite behavior.

The old adage that the bully wants to be loved or accepted is one example. Another is if your emotional needs were denied or abandoned, you may tend to be a giver to a fault, because you don't want to abandon another person. Each person is so unique in how they create their lost self that it helps to have a discussion to validate what it is for you. In fact, many people need help to discover their lost self because it isn't so obvious to most of us. The *Managing Your Crazy Self Workbook* is a guide created to help you discover your lost self and can be ordered at www.cerosinc.com.

Since there are two people in a marriage, there are two lost selves that need attention and healing. A couple's real challenge is that they each bring a different lost self they are reacting to that has to be dealt with in the relationship. Neither understands the other's unmet expectations being placed on them. Each one is connected to their own childhood. If left uncorrected, these issues will be passed on to their children as well; particularly in the way parents discipline their kids.

Each partner wants the other to give him or her the worth they haven't claimed for themselves. Disappointment, miscommunication, and resentment stemming from these unexamined and unspoken expectations multiply quickly without the partners realizing what is happening. The lost self will also flare up in workplace relationships.

That first unmet wound needs to be acknowledged so you can change its feeling and free yourself to achieve your potential. You will blindly spend the rest of your life reacting to emotions from your lost self until you do. But be encouraged; you are meant to heal. *Your brain is wired to create the problem from the instinctive and conscious brains maturing at different times, but it is also wired for you to resolve the issue using your conscious mind.* This is what self-development is. You learn about yourself and accept accountability to choose healthy perceptions and make good decisions. Your emotions and perceptions change accordingly. It isn't what happened to you that matters, it's how you handle it. And it matters for life.

I love the example of how those of us in the western world, particularly Americans, relate to Santa Claus. When we are born, we don't know Santa exists, so we don't believe in him. Later we hear about Santa and see him in malls and parades. We receive gifts from Santa. We come to believe in Santa. Then logic and reasoning kick in and we question how he can be everywhere in one night. How can he get down a chimney? How can he get all those presents on one sleigh? Eventually, we determine or accept that Santa isn't real; it is mom and dad giving us gifts. Now each of us has to decide: Am I excited I figured it out, or am I upset that people who love me lied to me? Most of us get past that pretty well. The real question is what we do with Santa when we have our own kids. For many, if not most, we become Santa. What a transition! This is a great example because it reflects the changes in perception we go through. The mind is amazing. But we can grow through these changes to arrive at a healthy understanding.

Your baseline insecurities get stored in a dormant state in childhood until you enter relationships later in life. Then they rise up with powerful emotions. You aren't sure why; you just feel it. You want something to happen but you want the other person to be responsible for making it happen. That is why it is called the lost self. You don't know that you are the one to make what you want happen for you. It's time to own it. You aren't a dependent child anymore.

One way to discover your lost self is to ask what you wanted as a child but didn't get. You may have wanted your mother's love, your father's approval, someone to believe in you, or something as simple as a horse (which would represent an emotional need you didn't get as a child). Most always, the lost self comes from a disappointment in a past relationship, or something you experienced from a past relationship that set an expectation. In the future, you will apply this expectation to someone else unconsciously. The *Managing Your Crazy Self Workbook* and accompanying coaching discussion will help you discover your lost self— if you need help.

We all have a lost self. It is a natural outcome of the delay in the development of your conscious mind while the instinctive brain is already mature at birth. Don't fear it. Think about it. Study it. Identify it if you can. Identify the specific something you want in your adult relationships and embrace it. Find a healthy perspective of how to give that to yourself. As a child, you are naturally dependent on your caregiver to meet your needs. As an adult, you are to learn to meet your own needs. When you are hurting, ask yourself, how can I be okay if someone else doesn't meet my need in the way I want?

The powerful damage of your unhealed lost self will lead you to give away your worth in the hope that someone else will provide your worth for you. You will become dependent on achieving goals or receiving accolades from others to be okay instead of just accepting yourself.

It is as if you wrote your worth on a 3x5 card and handed it over to someone you wanted affirmation or love from. They didn't want your worth. I jokingly say they lost your card in the wash. They were actually working on fulfilling their own lost self, not trying to take your worth away from you. You gave it away, innocently. It's time to take it back, if you haven't already.

If uncorrected, you will still expect someone else to give you worth today, be it your mate, partner, child, or boss. But they are not the correct person to give worth to you. You are to give it to yourself. That's why it is called "self-worth." The truth is that others cannot determine your true worth— only you can. You are to determine your worth and be happy with it! Take it back! Own it. Start today if you haven't done so before. It's helpful to recognize that other people are also looking to others to validate and heal their lost self. They want to earn or measure their worth by some external factor. In healthy thinking, no one wants to be responsible for someone else's self-worth.

I argued that I didn't have a lost self when I first read about it. But the more I studied, the more I realized I had to have one. The gap of time for the conscious mind to mature requires some unmet expectations to get stored in your memory. Once I decided to be open-minded about it, I saw so many new angles of looking at problems and finding solutions. Just as your body language will sell you out, so will your reactionary behaviors. Track reactions back to their source and you will find the unmet expectation. Healing the emotions from their source event will resolve insecurities and give you peace and confidence. You will claim your true worth.

Once you take your worth back you *begin* to be a healthy emotional you. You still have a lot of growing to do because you have to experience and store new memories of fulfilled expectations and successful actions to replace insecure reactions. When you recover your worth, you will trust yourself more and feel a new confidence that others will be drawn to. You can feel good about yourself and know why you should. It is a wonderful peace.

Chapter 11

Independence

Eventually, you move away from parental authority to be on your own.

I get to be me!

But you don't realize that you bring your baggage (old wounds) with you.

As you move out from authority to be on your own, you look forward to a new stage of life. You think you are free. In many ways, you are: but you are also about to discover that past emotions affect you today. Your old wounds can remain silent until you enter new relationships, but then they come roaring back to life. This is why getting to know someone can take time. You have to sort out your deep emotions. Your boyfriend, girlfriend, partner, or mate will need to sort theirs out as well. We grow in stages of development and awareness. Relationships teach us about ourselves.

One stage of development begins when kids have a job. I told my sons, "I love you greatly but would never want to deprive you of the opportunity to answer to someone else, show up and leave when they say, wear what they say, and do what they say. So, it is time to go get a job." Holding a job is a critical step in maturing from childhood dependence to healthy independence.

People of different generations tend to have particular emotional attributes. An HR professional told me that she is always interested in how much a student worked to pay for college. If they didn't have to work, they may not have developed a strong work ethic and thus have a sense of entitlement. She doesn't want to hire them and spend her company's resources on them while they develop a good work ethic. She would prefer a candidate who has already learned those values. Millennials grew up with instant everything at their fingertips—phone, email, text, Twitter, Google, movies, TV shows—and an attitude of if I don't get what I want from you; I will go find it on my own. Conversely, adults who grew up with parents of the Depression era and world wars tend to have greater respect for roles and authority. People from different countries also have different customs and expectations. All kinds of dynamics and experiences are ultimately recorded by our instinctive brain and set expectations that we bring to others.

And we wonder why others don't understand us!

Self-Therapy

Redirect your emotions throughout your day to sustain healthy cognitive decisions.

Understanding

Solutions for Your Mind

Redirect your emotions and connect with your conscious mind.

Chapter 12

The Solution

Not reacting to internal emotions *is* the first step. Then, make a simple, corrective, purposeful change. Redirecting the way you perceive a situation that triggers an emotional reaction is vital to healthy thinking.

Learn to change little things in the way you think. Redirecting is a conscious mind action that moves thoughts out of the defensive brain stem. When you change your thoughts, you change your emotions.

Turn down (redirect) the "wound tune" noise in your head.

Instead of reacting, find a positive thought or action—even *a single word or action* can make a big difference. For instance, when you meet someone, smile. When you smile, you will have a different disposition and cause different brain chemicals to flow.

The Power of One Simple Change

Instead of calling an inconsiderate driver a jerk (or worse), call him a genius. Changing this one word moves your thought process from your pea brain to your big brain. Using a positive word instead of a negative word will change the chemicals that are released throughout your body in that moment. Try it. You will feel the difference.

So, you can see that by changing one word or a simple action—a smile—you can change your whole mood and demeanor. That's why it's so helpful to call a "problem" an "opportunity," a "setback" a "discovery," or a "jerk" a "genius." You will be stimulating neurons in a healthy way. My, what power you have! *Change one word,* and you will feel the difference.

A bit of humor can also help. For instance, here's my go-to thought when I want to create a smile: I think of a little boy lying in the grass and laughing while a puppy is licking the boy's ear. Pick a thought that works for you. When you think of what makes you smile you will be moving your thoughts from your pea brain to your neocortex.

Here's another way to stop the cycle of noise in your head. At any moment in your day, you can make one simple change. To change your emotions, change your thoughts. To change your thoughts, change your setting. Change clothes (dress up one notch better than you feel), and you will feel better. Change the music that's playing to something upbeat that makes you want to get up and dance and sing. Change who you choose to talk to right now. Change your routine.

Test the power of one change for yourself. Change one thing each day consistently, and track it over a week. You'll see a difference. Here's how: Look back over last week, and determine one thing you can change. It could be exercising for five minutes each day. If you've decided to trim down, eat only half the food on your plate. Commit to making your first comment to each person a compliment, or commit to having only have one gripe a day.

Add a volume knob to your thoughts.

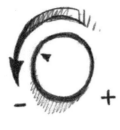

Volume

To reduce your emotional reactivity, turn down the volume of noise in your head. Just because your brain feeds you a thought doesn't mean you have to run with it or react to it. Don't feel that you have to be so mentally busy all the time. *Choose* your thoughts. Give yourself some breathing room, and move on with your day.

Chapter 13

It's Like Riding a Bicycle

You have already experienced successfully overcoming a challenging reaction by moving your thoughts from your brain stem to your neocortex. You just need to recognize your success and transfer that ability to other areas of your life. When did you do that? When you learned to ride a bike. You moved your thoughts from what if I fall (brain stem) to I know how to ride (neocortex).

Once you learned to ride a bicycle, what happened to the fear? Where did your fear go? The fear was replaced with new confidence.

The old emotion of fear in your memory that triggers brain stem reactions was rewritten with your new confidence to neocortex thinking. Now you *know* you can change a fear to confident success! You know how to think with a different part of your brain. You have proven to yourself that you can and no one can take that from you. Your brain correction works! You can heal an unhelpful perception, a fear, or a wound. Now transfer that ability to other areas of your life where you still feel fear or doubt. Address and change one at a time until you feel the confidence of being able to overcome any fear. It will change you forever.

Isn't it interesting that you never forget how to ride a bike?

Overcoming Struggles

Now when you see a bike you know you can ride it; there is no fear. You can remember the event of falling, but it doesn't hurt. That is because the thoughts are now drawn from a different part of your brain. The fearful emotion of falling was rewritten with the confidence of knowing how to ride. Fear is in ostrich thinking, not rhino thinking. Now pick the next area in your life you are going to conquer.

It is interesting how different people store their perceptions. If you ask two siblings about an event that they both clearly remember, each will tell you different things because they have different perceptions and emotions associated with it. If they talk about it together, they will gain new insights from each other—things they didn't realize about themselves and their interpretation of the event. The differing memories and interpretations of the event occur because your emotions are *unique to you.*

Emotions and events are recorded and stored separately, but they are linked. Every time you recall a memory, your brain seeks the corresponding emotion—*the feeling* associated with the memory. Here's the important thing to recognize: once you learn something new, you can *change your perception* of the memory and put it back into storage (memory) with a different viewpoint. You may not like something about someone. You may even generally dislike them until you find out something about them that you do like. It may be something as trivial as liking their shoes, or their laugh. You can like them because you like a part of them. You changed your perception because you have new knowledge (about their shoes or the way they laugh). This new knowledge enables you to like or at least tolerate them. You changed where you think your thoughts, which changed your biochemical and emotional reaction to them, and you created a new memory to draw on.

Pain from past events can lead to post-traumatic stress disorder. The event is long over, but the emotional pain is still alive. The instinctive brain will try to block the past pain from the conscious mind while at the same time holding on to that very pain. It's as if your brain doesn't want to deal with it. It seems hard to talk about. You won't recall exactly why you feel and behave the way you do. You just don't want to go there, because it is an uncomfortable feeling.

The inability to come to grips with this past pain can hinder your healthy thinking and negatively affect your current actions and relationships. The brain is wired for healing though—*if you choose it.* The old emotion simply needs a new perspective. There isn't any middle ground. You are either getting healthier or you are not.

When you hear yourself griping about something repeatedly, at some point it should give you a little inkling that you are doing this to yourself. Yes, work may be stressful, or family may be taking you for granted, or things may not be going well, but you can choose a better attitude by *changing one thing,* one thought, one word, or one action. Change one thing and get on with healthy living. Take charge of your life by choosing one productive thought at a time. I call this a healthy reboot moment. You can do it at any time of the day.

Chapter 14

How Healing Happens in Your Brain

Let's see how healing happens in the brain. The brain is designed to allow any emotion to heal by recording a new perception from new knowledge or experience to create a new emotion. This emotional perception change happens in the amygdala.

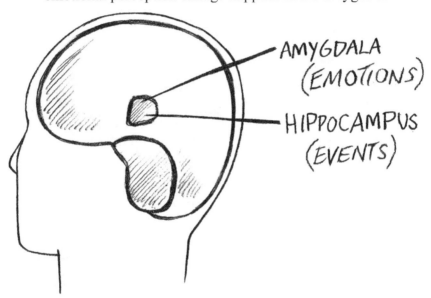

The amygdala stores emotions associated with an event, and the hippocampus stores the memory of the event.

The amygdala and hippocampus are connected in your memory bank. You can change the perception and emotion of an event. The memory of the event will not change.

You don't need to change the memories of events in your life to heal. For example, you remember falling off the bicycle, but once you know how to ride, you change the fear to confidence.

The **amygdala** stores the emotions associated with events.[5]

Example: As a child, a teacher may have shouted at you causing you to think, "Don't shout at me, I can't stand that." You may not recall exactly why you don't like people to raise their voice, but your amygdala remembers. A healthy new perspective is needed to replace this reaction.

The **hippocampus** stores the memory of the event (without the emotion).

Example: a jellyfish stung you once when in the ocean. So, now you think, I don't like going into the ocean. I always get stung by jellyfish. Now, the ocean reminds you of the event of getting stung, which your brain connects with the emotion of pain from the sting. You don't blame the jellyfish alone; now you blame the ocean.

Your brain can recall positive emotions and times in your life as well. You may see a drive-in fast food place and recall listening to a favorite song with your friends at lunch while in high school. Or, you may hear the song and then remember you went to lunch with your friends.

The memory of the event and the emotion of the event will trigger each other, though they are stored in separate places. You cannot change your memory of events. You can, however, change your emotions *about* the events. Changing emotions requires new knowledge, insight, or perspective. That is the key.

Here is an example: I asked a client to tell me about a time when he had a bad experience and got over it, and about another

---

5 John Bradshaw, *Bradshaw on: The Family: A New Way of Creating Self-Esteem* (Deerfield Beach, FL: Health Communications, 1988), 81.

time when he had a bad experience that he did not get over. He recalled taking some friends to a bar for drinks after a ball game. He was going to drive them home afterward, only to discover that his car had been towed. He was angry and embarrassed to say the least and it bothered him for some time. About six months later, he realized the potential disaster he had avoided. If he had driven while intoxicated, he could have wrecked his car, hurt or killed someone, or gotten a DUI and damaged his career opportunities. He now feels that someone or something—God's grace or a guardian angel—was looking out for him. "That's a great example of changing your perspective of a bad event," I told him. "Now tell me about one you haven't resolved."

He told me he could easily identify that one. He was going to propose to a girl he had dated for over a year. Two weeks before he planned to ask her, she dumped him for another guy. "I still have trouble wanting to date again," he told me. I replied immediately with "I know what happened!" "What?" he asked. "Tell me." I told him it was simple: "Your girl got towed!" He paused a bit and I let him think on it. I can still see the look on his face as the tension left his brow and passed down through his face in release. He said, "If I had married her, it would have been a bad relationship and would have likely broken up later." He paused. "Thank you," he said. "I don't think I would have ever looked at it that way." He could perceive the event differently now.

Emotions derive from perceptions and can be changed. Events are facts.

The amygdala and hippocampus work independently but are linked inside the limbic system. The key thing to understand is when the brain records new experiences and new emotions old emotions associated with old events are displaced. To heal a traumatic or wounding experience, we need a new perspective or new knowledge. You can heal with a positive correction of experience or knowledge, and it doesn't have to hurt.

Every time you learn something new and productive, you're using the neocortex (big brain). The big brain creates a new positive emotion that gets recorded in the limbic system (pea

67

brain). If you fall off the horse, you need to get back on. It is amazing how the old emotional wound tunes play constantly in your instinctive brain and daily affect your emotions and reactions. Not changing old emotions leaves them entrenched, and old wounds will affect and harm current and future relationships because they are not healed with a healthy perspective.

We often bury wounded emotions when what we need to do is discover them, talk about them, and learn a new healthy perspective about the event. Instead of beating yourself up when you notice the old patterns emerging, pat yourself on the back. Why? Because awareness is the first step to making the changes you desire. Gain confidence as you achieve small victories along the way.

Just because an old wound is buried doesn't mean it can't or shouldn't be healed. Find a new perspective and you will change the emotion. Negative emotions drain energy and create unhealthy stress. Productive emotions create healthy energy and relieve stress. You are wired to heal. Learn how, trust you can do it, and practice!

Chapter 15

Unhealthy Versus Healthy Loops

There are unhealthy loops of thought, and there are healthy loops of thought. Healthy loops bypass the brain stem. Avoid brain stem thinking. Redirect quickly to rhino thoughts in your conscious mind.

Simplified Version

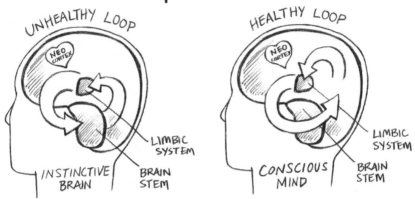

Unhealthy Loop of Reactionary Thoughts

Healthy Loop of Thoughts

When thoughts go from the limbic system to the brain stem you react in fight, flight, or freeze behaviors, which are then recorded back in the limbic system, which then triggers recurring emotions that lead back to fight, flight, or freeze again. This is an unhealthy loop. If you don't break the cycle, you stay stuck in a loop that bypasses the conscious mind and is locked in fight, flight, or freeze reactions. Healthy decisions won't even come up for consideration. The result is that your behaviors will deteriorate and you'll experience undesirable consequences in your life and relationships.

Healthy Loop of Calm, Organized Thoughts

When thoughts from the limbic system get redirected to the conscious mind, however, they bypass the brain stem. Now you avoid fight, flight, or freeze and a healthy action gets recorded, changing your memory to include a new experience to draw from. Learning a new behavior or skill takes practice. Don't get discouraged if you find yourself defaulting to negative thoughts and poor attitudes. Stay positive and take the steps needed to create a healthy attitude. Reboot often to stop reactionary emotions from controlling you.

Trying something new can be exciting and may either block or trigger some Alerts! New events can cause your instinctive brain to scour your memory for old wounding experiences to keep you protected, which may make you unnecessarily cautious. Once your brain perceives danger, your emotions will run higher because of the chemicals that are released. Emotions trigger chemicals and chemicals trigger emotions. Healthy thinking produces healthy chemicals.

Even when you try to move forward with healthy decisions to exercise or eat better, your instinctive brain will automatically react with old Alerts! that trigger old reactions. Be aware that this will happen, and be ready. At first, you are excited about making a positive change, but then your brain recalls something and you think, well, I'm too tired, or maybe next time. Redirect those old reactions to stay productive. These thought patterns in your mind are the reason old habits are difficult to change. Your brain calls up old memories and reactions. You have to create new ones that replace the old ones. Keep initiating healthy change and keep rebooting all the Alerts! Don't feel guilty if your efforts don't pay off at first; guilt is another old emotional reaction. You are experiencing the steps of creating change.

A client in her sixties kept pointing out that she didn't like to go places. She repeated this often. Instead of addressing each event and asking why each place caused her hesitation, I recalled that she had shared a very bad experience about walking to school in kindergarten. Her brain was associating going to any new environment with that early frightening experience, which made her reluctant to go anywhere in the present. She carried that fear with her for decades. She was amazed when I brought it to her attention. She said no one had ever recognized that connection despite years of therapy. Now she understands her emotional reaction, catches herself, reboots with healthy thoughts, and gets out and about.

Often positive opportunities create fearful emotions. A job interview can trigger insecurity. Going to a new business or social event can create uneasiness. A guy talking to a new girl may feel hesitant. Where do these emotions come from? They are deep-seated from your life experiences. They are myths. They don't have to apply today. After all, who told you to feel that way? The new opportunity triggers old emotions. Redirect your thoughts and choose a perspective that will give you the confidence you need.

Three Steps for Making a Change

Recognize that when you want to create a new behavior, there are three steps you must go through. You can't skip them. They are required:

1. Think it until you do it. (Focus on the change you want to make until it becomes natural.).
2. Keep doing it until it becomes automatic.
3. When it becomes a habit, others will compliment your achievement.

If you decide to eat less by only eating half portions, you may find yourself forgetting or simply not following through at times. Keep thinking about your action plan until you are doing it more often than not. Soon enough you will do it most of the time, and eventually you will do it naturally. Before too long, someone will say, "Your neck looks thinner. You're looking good."

When you want to make a change, the best possible approach is to recognize the root insecurity holding you back and find a way to change your perception at that source. Once you do, your instinctive brain will change all the subsequent Alerts! for the associated memory. Don't just keep treating the symptoms. Treat the source and your brain will apply the new perceptions to other memories.

Take charge of your emotions. Choose how you want to feel. Find a method that works for you. Acknowledge old feelings and then make a change in your viewpoint. There are many methods; you just need to find which ones work best for you. Be willing to customize to make it fun and interesting. In chapter 18, you'll find twelve easy-to-apply Take Charge Rhino Tips to help you take charge of your life.

Chapter 16

Managing the Cycle of Emotions

Do you ever feel like the ostrich on the wheel? Your conscious mind is the control lever to manage your instinctive brain's reactions of thoughts, emotions, and unwanted behaviors.

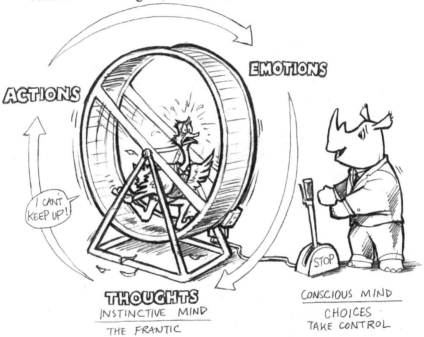

Emotions continuously trigger thoughts, which trigger actions, which trigger emotions, until you stop the cycle.

The instinctive brain will never tell the conscious mind to pull the lever and slow things down. You have to be aware and choose to do healthy things. Practice daily. Pay attention to when you feel upset or react to something. Ask yourself, why did I need to react? Why not just be aware? Even when others mention a fault or offer a you a suggestion, you may not be able to accept it when you are caught up in the emotional spin cycle of your instinctive brain. You will most likely ignore or deny the issue. Decide to step back, be calm, and think clearly.

I had been working long hours for a few years, with a long commute, raising three kids while my spouse worked overseas for most of each year. A friend told me I needed a weeklong vacation to just get away and relax. "There is just no way. I don't see how I can do that," I replied defensively. However, I was able to hear it. I realized that they must have seen some stress in me I didn't see to tell me I needed a vacation. Finally, nine months later, I did take a week off. I went to a relaxing outdoor training camp setting in the mountains with a group of friends and did almost nothing for a week. I had no job duties, no kids, and no home chores. I felt myself detox from all my tensions. I will never forget that release. When I get stressed now I quickly remember that vacation and allow myself to feel like I am in that relaxed setting.

Use new methods and skills to address issues instead of letting your reactive emotions get the best of you. See the following charts for some examples of triggers and methods.

Triggers that lead you to react:	
Someone using a negative tone	Repetitive mistakes
Loud talking, yelling	Repeated problems
Hearing music you don't like	Bad drivers
Someone being late	Interruptions

Methods that keep, or redirect you to being calm:	
Saying a funny word or line from a movie	Calling a friend
Changing your setting to a peaceful one	Long slow breaths
Doing something nice for someone instead of reacting poorly	A great song
Writing yourself a brief email to vent	Healthy hobbies
Caring for someone less fortunate	Contacting a mentor or advisor

Healing the Mind

Healing happens when new knowledge or insight changes your perspective.

The ostrich sees the picture as something scary.
The rhino says let's look at it a different way!

Once you learn to change your perceptions, you can take charge of your thoughts at any time. You are the only one who can give yourself peace and healthy thoughts.

Often the solution is as simple as finding a surprising new angle you hadn't thought of before. You don't have to change your values; just be open to new insights.

Understanding the Mind in

Your Relationships

Your crazy comes out in interactions with others!

Chapter 17

Four Key Relationships

Old emotions surface in your new relationships.

There are four critical relationship areas where past emotions stored in your instinctive brain manifest in your behavior and communication. These relationships are with yourself, your mate, your children, and your coworkers—particularly those who have authority over you or over whom you have authority.

a. **Yourself**

b. **Your Mate**

c. **Your Child(ren)**

d. **Your Coworkers**

Addressing the many factors involved in these different relationships is beyond the scope of this book. The purpose here is simply to identify these four categories so that you are aware of them. Managing your thoughts and emotions will naturally improve each of these relationships because changing your own perceptions, emotions, and behaviors will change how others respond to you. Change yourself and others will change the way they respond to you.

Visit www.cerosinc.com for blogs and videos about how to improve your relationships.

a. Yourself

Your first relationship is with yourself. Talk to yourself in a healthy way.

Self-Talk

Talk to yourself (your instinctive brain): Say, "You can relax! I got this. I've decided to change that perceived NEED to a WANT. So I'm okay now."

No one can manage your mind for you. It only takes a few seconds to pause, recognize your tendencies, and redirect to something productive. You can maintain healthy thinking even when those around you are expressing unhealthy thinking. To do so you have to overcome your instinctive emotional Alerts!

Often you think of something as if it is an absolute NEED. It isn't. Change your perceived NEED to a WANT. For example, instead of saying I NEEDED to win a race or stay married, I recognized that I WANTED to win the race, I WANTED to be loved, and I WANTED to stay married. When you change your NEED to a WANT, it changes your perception and the chemicals

81

released in your brain and body. Changing how you think changes your mind, body, and spirit. Coaching and the *Managing Your Crazy Self Workbook* will help you shorten this learning curve and make these changes quickly.

A 65-year-old client told me she was born an alcoholic because her mother drank throughout the pregnancy. She had a great sense of humor and joked that she was on the bottle from birth. She didn't literally start drinking until she was a teenager, but by age 35, she realized she was an alcoholic. Her drinking had dramatic effects on her marriage and kids, and she and her husband eventually divorced. She realized she needed to get sober and with the help of Alcoholic Anonymous (AA), she did (and she still attends AA meetings to this day). She was very bright; however, she still had addictive tendencies and became an overeater. By the time she was ready to retire, she decided to have weight loss surgery. I met her at a bariatric support group session I was leading. She told me she was doing well but could use some help answering some questions she could never resolve. She gained a lot of insights during our sessions and was making good progress. One day she called me to reach out feeling her old emotions were consuming her and needing help to break free from old patterns of thoughts and behaviors (I invite all of my clients to call me for help in their dark hour).

She had never called before, and I could tell she was quite agitated and demanding. She had just come back from a very stressful visit to her out-of-state family and was desperately craving a cookie. "What do I do?" she asked. As I listened I began thinking quickly to myself; okay, she is very upset, and she's never called before so this is a crisis moment. When an alcoholic takes one sip, they end up drinking an entire bottle. If she eats a cookie, will she eat a whole box? So, I asked her, "Are you going to eat a whole box of cookies?" She replied, "It's much worse than that. I am dressed to go for a walk at the mall. I am fooling myself by pretending to go exercise when what I am going to do is walk by the Cookie Factory. The first time I pass by, I'm going to smell those cookies and get all worked up. By the second or third time I pass the Cookie Factory I will be all crazy and buy a box of them." Tracking with her, I said, "You will go home, eat the whole box,

82

throw them up because your stomach is too small to handle it, and feel terribly guilty and ashamed that you did it again." "Yes!" she said intensely, "And I hate that, so I am calling you! I am headed out the door and I stopped to call you. What do I do?"

"Let me think a minute," I said. "This is like two kids getting naked in the back seat of a car about to have sex when one of them suddenly thinks of the consequences." Obviously frustrated, she said, "WHAT does THAT have to do with me?" "You need to put a rubber on the cookie," I said. After a brief pause, she burst out laughing. She laughed so hard she couldn't breathe. After about a minute she finally caught her breath and was able to pause between bursts of laughter to say, "I... don't think... I will ever...look at a cookie the same again." "Good," I said. "Next problem?" She has since visited her family several times without any breakdown crises afterward.

Another client I worked with had been raised with a lot of abuse. She externalized her worth to her work and became a workaholic to the point of physically and emotionally exhausting herself every day. Her job at a hospital required her to qualify for an important national certification. It was a huge yearlong project that required detailed documentation, and she had very limited support to help her with the additional work. By the time she got home at 9 p.m. each night, she was an emotional wreck. Having left home as a teenager, she was incredibly street-smart. Like many of us, she needed help managing her weaknesses in order to capitalize on her strengths. One night she called to tell me how much effort she was putting in at work only to have everything go wrong. Since I had worked with her for a few months, I was aware of all of that and realized she had again worked past dinner without eating and was venting in overdrive.

As I was reminding her that she hadn't stopped at 5 or 6 p.m. to get a change of scenery and a bite to eat, she changed topics. She replied, "And tomorrow I have to get a haircut, but I hate getting a haircut. They always cut it wrong and I have to live with it until the next time. I just hate it." At this point, she was bawling. This confirmed to me that she needed a mental reboot, so

I asked if she ever showed her hairdresser what she didn't want? She paused a moment, totally changing her demeanor, and said calmly, "No." I went on, "Why not take picture of what you want, and what you don't want, and show her?" She said, "I never thought of that."

Keying on her wonderfully intelligent street smarts, I then suggested, "And when you go in, first ask her for her driver's license." "Why would I do that?" she asked. Now she was back to a very normal tone instead of crying. I said, "You can tell her that you are trusting her to cut your hair. If she does it wrong you will cut up her driver's license. If you have to grow out a bad haircut, she will have to get a new driver's license. Then you'll be even." She laughed and said, "I don't think I can do that." "You don't have to," I replied, "All you have to do is think it, and you will have changed your thoughts to the conscious mind. You will be fine."

She got it. Most amazing to me is that she never called again in a moment of despair. She went on to finish her work campaign successfully. Soon afterwards, she found a less stressful job and married within a year.

b. Your Mate

Identifying your mate. We can all dream, can't we?

Correct your self-created image of your mate.

You create an expectation of what you think you want your mate to be by gathering information from different sources: traits you consciously decide you desire, what you saw in your parents or caregiver, what you see in other couples, and what you actually see in your mate. Harville Hendrix calls the unconscious image of your ideal mate your "imago."[6] Essentially, your imago is the unrealistic list of expectations you want your mate to meet.

One day the reality hits that your mate isn't ever going to meet your imago list. This is when the relationship begins! It is

---

[6] Hendrix, 38.

best to love the one you are with and get rid of your list of expectations. Otherwise, you get rid of your mate and take your unrealistic list into the next relationship.

At the same time your mate has their own imago list they want you to meet. An authentic, healthy relationship begins when you discard your list and love your mate.

These principles apply when addressing normal relationships, not relationships that involve abuse, addictions, or other disorders.

Communicating with Your Mate's Mind

Understanding how your minds interact.

Couples love each other in their conscious mind.
But their instinctive brains don't date!

Reactive emotions come from the instinctive brain and surface in your words and behaviors. They include thoughts like I can't stand it when you do that; you don't care about me; or you are driving me crazy. If you communicate from your reactive emotions, you are talking to your mate from your instinctive brain. This will not be productive! It will trigger defensive reactions, not love.

Say positive words and take positive actions when you least feel like it. This approach will *redirect your emotions* from your instinctive brain to your conscious mind. For example, when you know you are too wiped out to have a productive conversation with your mate, try saying, "I'm tired, and you have worked hard today, too. Can we address this tomorrow when I'm in a better state of mind?" You can *also redirect your mate's emotions* by moving their thoughts from their instinctive brain to their conscious mind.

Saying, "Let's each tell each other about our day for 10 or 15 minutes, and then let's do something fun together."

Couples are rewarding to work with but more challenging; because with a couple there are three clients: each individual and then the two together. Working out issues in your relationship with a mate is where you challenge yourself the most. You learn the most about yourself when you live with someone else and care for their needs as well as your own. Each partner needs to "fix" themselves first, which means understanding where their emotional perceptions and wounds originated in order to make healthy adjustments in expectations and behaviors. It is a slower process, but the rewards last a lifetime when you get it right.

Each couple is different in their needs and wants, and often unconscious of the source issue they are most emotional about. The instinctive brain often masks the core issue from the conscious mind, and each partner transfers expectations onto their mate as a result. The mate will never be able to resolve this unspoken expectation because they can't go inside their partner's brain to address it. Instead, the brain stem generates unhealthy coping mechanisms (fight, flight or freeze), and people often add in bad habits to compensate for the love they want but are missing or blocking. Even if one partner resolves their deep internal wound, the other still needs to do their own work. Longstanding relationship issues are solvable if each partner is willing to face their core issue. The media often reports that money is a root cause for divorce, but my experience is that this is not true. Money is an easy target, but underneath is an unmet emotional expectation or a perception that can be addressed and dealt with in healthy ways.

I worked with a couple who had both been married previously. Both are very good people; however, he is a perfectionist, and she is defensively independent. Their behavior styles were both assertive towards problems. They were trying so hard to experience love. But their perceptions were based on past unmet expectations, and their behavior styles were so strong that spontaneous combustion happened often. As much as they didn't like arguments, they couldn't seem to avoid them. Life was measured from one argument to the next.

Discussions led to the discovery that he couldn't love himself because he was locked in his past unmet emotional needs, which played in his instinctive brain continuously. It was easier for him to demand perfection from his wife than to love himself. For her part, she was truthful to a fault, often pointing out his flaws and mistakes even when she didn't need to. Trying to get at the issue in a humorous way, I told her she had truth Tourette syndrome, and she agreed. Her strategy was to build a wall of truth around her because she was vulnerable inside. It was easier for her to protect herself at all costs than to be vulnerable, even if it meant hurting the one she wanted love from. So, she would point out his faults, which made him want to prove he was right or she was wrong. Off they went, shooting mortar at each other until they were exhausted. It can be very difficult to overcome emotional Alerts! and choose healthy actions, but they are learning and continue to work on their marriage. The key is to not react to instinctive brain Alerts! (old habits) but instead to pause, reboot, and then act on your desired outcomes.

c. Your Child(ren)

Your parenting style is shaped by emotions from your lost self (what you wanted as a child but didn't get) and what you think it means to be a good parent. These factors combine to determine how you relate to and discipline your child. Some parents become very strict, while others become overly permissive. The instinctive brain led your parents to subconsciously apply their childhood emotions to raising you, and your children will do the same with their children.

That's a great idea son, but first check your chores list and see if anything needs to be done.

A healthier approach is to understand and fulfill your role as a parent first, and then apply your perspective and personality to your role. Your child needs a confident parent first, and then they want a friendship with you as the unique person you are.

Be sure to recognize your child's individuality as a gift. Don't try to make them into someone they are not because that is who you want them to be. You can easily see a perception change in the way grandparents treat grandchildren differently than they treated their children. Often they are much easier on their grandchildren than they were on their children.

A father called me looking for help with his 16-year-old son. He asked how could we work with his son without isolating the son and making him feel everything was his fault. I suggested we assess the whole family, both parents and the two teenage sons and he thought that was a great idea. I asked if the mom and the son were struggling and he said yes; in fact, that was where the worst communication was happening.

After assessing the whole family, I recognized the mom was very strict and demanding with both sons. She was very loving, but had a lot of rules about how the sons were to do things. The 16-year-old son was a creative thinker and tended to seek forgiveness rather than ask permission. He needed to learn the consequences of his actions by experience and not by theory. This drove his mother crazy, because that wasn't how she operated. One day I asked her why he had to come home from school at 3:30 p.m., put his shoes by the door and books on the counter, and then do his homework immediately. We had completed several sessions to help her understand herself better, and at this point, it hit her. "Oh my, I have become my mother," she said tearfully. "I am requiring these things of him because this is what my mom wanted from me." I said to her, "Having your kids do everything perfectly is never going to give you the approval you want from your mom."

As a child, she had based her worth on pleasing her mom. She would do everything just right as a child to gain her mom's approval and now she expected her kids to do the same. Her older son had a similar disposition and was fine with her approach, so she had no problem with him. However, the 16-year-old wasn't wired to respond to that kind of management. "So what do I do?" she asked me in resignation. "Let him do things on his own schedule. He will make mistakes, but he will learn from them," I said. *"You're telling me to teach my child to fail?"* she asked, obviously frustrated with me. *"Not teach him to fail,"* I said, *"Just allow him to fail. He's a bright kid and will not likely make the same mistake twice."* Still doubtful, she asked me for a specific activity to test out this approach. *"Let him wash one load of clothes each week,"* I suggested. *"He'll break the washer,"* she quickly replied. *"Can you afford another washer?"* I asked. *"Yes,"* she said, shrugging her shoulders. *"Well, washers are difficult to break and I don't think he will break it. I certainly don't think he will break it twice. If he does, you can have him help pay for the second one.* I explained that it was better that he learn from his mistakes while he lived at home than to fail in college and not have a clue how to manage that. *"Even if he is late to school too much, or fails a class, he can take a summer school course. Let him learn from his consequences,"* I encouraged. I even suggested she consider leaving the house early each morning, leaving him to get himself off to school each day while she exercised or had breakfast with a friend. That way she wouldn't be there to react to his every move.

She agreed to let him get up, take the dog out, and drive to school without her oversight each morning. She also agreed to let him do his homework on his schedule, though she did restrict the hours he was allowed to use the computer.

The new plan paid off for both mom and son. The new freedoms helped him to feel more independent and gain trust in himself as he made decisions and was accountable for his choices. As a result, he willingly opened up to discuss grades, problems, and girlfriends with his parents rather than hide those issues for fear of judgment and getting yelled at.

The son is now in college and doing well. He says he realizes now that his parents gave him a lot more freedom than his peers had. One day he texted his mom to say all his roommate's laundry came out pink in the wash while he knew how to take care of his laundry. I think he's going to be okay.

d. Your Coworkers

There are three perceptions that your instinctive brain will tend to apply in your work environment (unless you have corrected them): a. You view your boss as a parental authority. b. You view yourself as a parental authority over employees who report to you. c. You view peers and customers as friends, unless they are in competition with you, because there is no authority in those relationships. Authority dynamics tend to trigger brain stem protections.

You're doing a great job! Tell me how you do it? (Remember, you are always talking to the other person's ostrich.)

Remember to speak to others from your calm conscious mind so they will not react, but will respond to you without fight, flight, or freeze thinking. Be sure to keep recognition and appreciation of an employee as a person separate from appreciation of their work performance.

So often, I find that supervisors are wonderful with their employees, but have a victim mindset when addressing someone who has authority over them. They need to view themselves as equally worthy and confident when addressing those in authority over them. This is another area where unmet emotional needs surface and lead to subconscious reactions that don't give us the feelings or results we really want.

I was called in to work with a team of nursing directors at a hospital. They had just come out of a staff meeting, and one woman was extremely upset. She was ranting about every problem she could think of. Everyone else sat quietly, waiting to see what I would say. I knew she was too stressed to discuss problematic issues at the moment, so to calm her down I asked, "Vicki, what is your love language?" She quickly retorted, "Oh I can show love all kinds of ways." "No," I clarified, "What makes you feel loved?" She just stood there speechless, staring at me. I said, "Your love bucket is empty." Her fellow director elbowed her and said, "Your love bucket is full of rocks!"

I loved hearing that because it told me this team had enough camaraderie to be able to talk to each other like that.

Communicating with someone using their love language is a good way to redirect their thoughts to their conscious mind and fill their love bucket at the same time. In a work setting, you don't have to love everyone, but you do need to appreciate them. People are more engaged and do more when they feel appreciated.

In his book *The Five Love Languages*, Gary Chapman explains that people have different preferences for how they receive love. Some experience love most deeply when they receive words of affirmation; others need touch, acts of service, gifts, or quality time the most. We tend to show love the way we want it rather than the way others want it. Learn to share appreciation in the way others want to receive it.

One director-level client was a great performer, but had difficulty with staff relationships. Upper management wanted to promote him, but couldn't unless he improved his communication and relationship skills. Assessments revealed he was intensely perfectionistic, much more so than most. To paint a picture for him, I told him he was on the edge of the galaxy, not anywhere near the middle. He could see everyone in the middle but they saw him way out there all by himself. He nodded. I gave him a few new methods to communicate better with his staff each day. I like to use simple techniques that get a maximum return. I suggested he make a list of each staff person and his or her child or pet's name. I told him to skip asking how the staff person was, but to just ask something about the child or pet by name. He looked at me curiously and asked, "Why would I do that?" "Because that is why they are working for you," I replied. He nodded again.

A week later, I met with him again and asked if he had used any of the techniques. He said yes and that the responses were very interesting, in fact, one person "unresigned." I said, "That's unusual," and asked him to tell me more. He reported that this employee came to him and said, "Something is different. If it's real I want to stay." "Oh!" I said, "Do you know what she was saying?" He shook his head no. "She was saying you were the problem. She likes the job, pay, benefits, and the commute, but she didn't feel valued or have a connection with you, her boss." Most people leave a job when they don't feel valued. He nodded yes, indicating that made sense to him. He became a believer in the value of communicating better with his staff and was soon promoted.

A third situation involved a director who was not communicating upward. He was great with his staff but when dealing those in authority over him, he would switch to a victim mentality. I call this the hourglass syndrome. The individual is in the middle where the sand falls from the top to the bottom. They manage people wonderfully when they have authority over them. But when addressing anyone with authority over them, they became very self-protective and offered minimal communication. I drew that diagram for him and explained he was a good director with people below him but was starving those above him of the very information he willingly shared with those below him; the sands of information were not flowing upward. He had never

95

realized that about himself before. We worked on ways to make changes and increase how often he communicated to people above him, and he was recognized for his efforts. He had been defaulting to defensive brain stem thinking when addressing those in authority but learned to switch to using his neocortex (conscious mind).

Four Coaching Situations for Coworkers

When I work with organizations to coach their staff the underlying problem usually falls in one of four categories. Once I recognize the problem, it's usually not difficult to apply the right solution.

1. Does the person understand their role or position?

Too often, a person is being driven by their emotions or past wounding instead of fulfilling the role of their position. For example, employees want their supervisors to be an effective boss more than they want the boss to be a friend. Think about being a good boss first, and being personable second. Learn to fulfill your role with good management and leadership skills and let go of reactionary emotions. When you embody your role properly, your staff can understand and fulfill their role.

2. Does the person understand how to communicate with different personality types?

There are many personality types in the workplace and each requires different communication methods. Learning how to talk to someone in their style makes communication much more effective than requiring them to talk to you in your style. There are many behavior style assessments available and most include very useful information about what motivates individuals as well. Find one that works. Then learn it, use it, and become good at adapting your communication to the other person's behavior style. I love and use the DISC behavior style assessment for many reasons: People can readily understand DISC, it is very accurate and reliable, and the report content is wonderfully easy-to-use. It also differentiates between your natural style and the style you adopt when you are under stress. This tool is difficult to skew and the graphs are rich in insights. Please note that DISC is out of patent and many companies have created their own versions. Unfortunately, some focus more on marketing than on statistical validity. The result is that clients end up using the tool in inappropriate ways that aren't helpful. Be sure to double-check any tool you choose for statistical validity.

No single personality assessment covers every aspect of personality. The scientific community has developed ways to measure many important facets of personality and behavior over the last few decades. These facets include behavior style, motivators, competencies, learning style, love language, and emotional intelligence. Each of these aspects of an employee's abilities, thoughts, and behavior affects performance, whether for good or bad, and that translates very quickly into dollars.

(You can inquire about and order assessments at www.cerosinc.com.)

3. Does the person have the skills needed for the job?

Very good employees are often promoted into management because they are wonderful performers. However, many of them haven't had the opportunity to develop the skills needed to manage and lead others. These skill deficiencies affect the person who was promoted, the staff they are to lead, and the manager they report to. Poor management and leadership negatively influence company culture and employee trust, directly reducing productivity and the return of investment on salaries paid to employees. Promoting people to a level of incompetency is not productive, and is much more expensive than the budget line items indicate. For this reason, training and coaching are needed at every level. If you are the CEO or president, what level of performance do you want from your employees for the dollars paid to them? Would it influence your bottom line if you could improve performance? Knowing which staff to work with to gain the greatest return is critical to positively leveraging your human resource investment.

4. Does the person bring an emotional wound, disorder, or dysfunction to the job with them?

Sometimes the problem is that someone cannot leave their personal issues at the door when they come to work. They need help managing their personal problem so they and the company can benefit from their valuable skills and abilities. Their emotional wounds and unhelpful perceptions surface in their work relationships and hinder their performance.

Wouldn't it be great if we could all write our personal issues on a card and leave them in an envelope at the door when we go in to work? Then we could be the effective professionals we were trained and educated to be from 8 a.m. to 5 p.m. When we left work to go home, we could pick up our issues and go knock our lights out with them. Better yet, we could swap with someone and pick up his or her problems! But the truth is that no one is likely to want to trade for someone else's problems; this truth reveals that we tend to nurture our problems rather than resolve them.

Once you can identify which situation is the problem area in the workplace, the treatment is simple. The more difficult part is getting the manager or employee to experience success and gain trust in their decision-making.

Too often, a seminar makes for a great day, but staff go back to business as usual the next day. Training without personal coaching doesn't pay off if the candidate is in survival mode. Buy-in is critical to successful growth and development. Participants must allow the coach to hold them accountable for coaching to be effective. As great as online classes are, they don't typically converse with participants, heal past wounds, or effectively challenge staff to achieve their potential.

Managing Emotions from Your Mind in

Daily Life

Simple tips to manage your crazy into success!

How You React to Your Emotions During the Day

Reacting leads to frantic chaos and disorganization.

Instinctive Brain

What to do?! What to do?! What to do?!

How to Manage Your Emotions During the Day

Intentional thoughts give order to your life and emotions.

Conscious Mind

Don't let your ostrich throw you off.

Chapter 18

Twelve Take Charge Rhino Tips to Help Manage and Change Your Emotions

Do you ever wish you could catch yourself before you said or did something you regret? I have great news for you—you can! When you practice the steps below, you move your thoughts from your instinctive brain to your conscious mind and change how you respond to everyday situations. Consistently doing one small thing right can change your life.

Let's look at the twelve rhino tips to help you manage your emotions using your conscious mind.

1. Name your crazy self.

 Take a moment to name your crazy self, that is your undesirable emotions and behaviors. When you name something, you claim authority over it. People name their dogs, their cars, their kids, their company, etc. When you name your crazy self you take authority over the instinctive, reactive part of your brain. Choose a name that will make you smile every time you use it. You might choose a character from a favorite TV show, movie, or cartoon. One client called herself Wile E. Coyote, as in the Looney Tunes character who was always trying to catch the Road Runner. Naming gives you a release valve to redirect from reactionary emotions to your favorite character, and smile instead of getting upset. This is an effective way to free you from your instinctive brain and engage your conscious mind. Now you can choose to take a healthy action. Giving your crazy self a name that makes you laugh removes fear and the feeling of being threatened.

An attorney I worked with called his stressed-out work persona Kramer, like the character from the TV show Seinfeld. Thinking of Kramer always made him laugh. As he drove home, he would transition by consciously deciding to leave Kramer at work and be his real self (a husband and dad) when he walked into the house. He found that practice helped him escape from work pressures when he was at home. When he asked me what he should do when he fell back into stress mode at home, I told him to tell Kramer he wasn't scheduled to see him until his appointment tomorrow at 8:30 a.m. Kramer would just have to wait until then. He laughed and said, "Okay, I get it."

Another client who worried too much about everything loved Tim Conway as Mr. Tudball on the Carol Burnett Show. He would picture his crazy self as Mr. Tudball playing golf (because he loved golf) and it would snap his emotions back to a healthy, fun attitude. He would imagine Mr. Tudball saying "Misses uh Wiggins, would you uh hand me uh the four iron." Doing so redirected him back to a relaxed, fun, conscious mind perspective when he felt his insecurities rise. This visualization freed him from feelings of abandonment or being alone. He would laugh and remember he is okay and can love himself. He said, "You know, I can do that. I feel the difference. It's funny that it's so simple."

A single mom worked as an administrative assistant, but found it very stressful because her personality profile didn't fit the job. I told her I respected her making a living as a single mom but that she should consider jobs that fit her style. Her main complaint was that people came into the office to gripe to the CEO all day and called relentlessly to follow up. "Sometimes I just want to meet them in the parking lot and settle it," she said. I asked if she had done any theatre, and she said she had loved it in high school. "Good," I said, "Then have Irene answer the phone." She looked perplexed and asked who Irene was. "Anyone you want her to be. But she should be a person who loves customer service, gets problems resolved, and makes people happy. Then when you hang up, go back to being you," I said. "I love it!" she said, slapping the desk. The next week I dropped by and asked how Irene was doing. Her associate said, "Oh she has five different characters answering the phone now."

Your crazy self isn't the real you. Your crazy self is the emotions from your instinctive brain's computer that generates issues from past wounds and unresolved expectations. Name your crazy emotions, redirect your thoughts, laugh, and give yourself permission to think healthy thoughts instead. Be free from reactive emotions that don't serve you. You acquired these unmet expectations along the way. They don't have to control you.

2. Limit yourself to one gripe (angry thought, worry, or anxiety) per day.

Only allow one gripe, worry, or stressful experience per day. You only get one gripe, so make it a good one. Make it worthy! If something upsets you, first decide if this is going to be your one gripe today. If so, the rest of the day is a gripe-free day; go enjoy it. If you decide a gripe isn't that bad, then you can't stress or get upset yet. Be ready to catch yourself when you think that makes me so angry, or I'm so tired of this, or whatever your complaint is, and decide if that is your one gripe for the day. You will soon laugh at your problems because you'll be dealing with them more objectively.

One time I told my son, "Oops, that's my gripe for today," and he replied, "Dad, that was your third gripe. You don't get any more gripes until Wednesday." It's interesting how we influence others. They are paying attention even when we don't think so.

3. Schedule acting on emotional stress for tomorrow.

Acknowledge your one gripe or stress point today, but act on it tomorrow. Just because you decided what your one gripe is going to be today doesn't mean you have to act on it immediately. Schedule taking any action for tomorrow. Be specific about when the time will begin and end. For example, instead of getting upset and saying, "That makes me so mad!" you could say, "I will be mad tomorrow at 9 a.m. I am not going to let that ruin my day today." Tomorrow at 9 a.m. be mad—really mad—for one minute. Then move on. At 9:01 a.m. stop being mad and go enjoy your day. Delaying until tomorrow limits your negative thoughts in the moment. So often though, once you sleep on it, you forget to be mad. So, maybe it wasn't so important after all, but just an emotional false Alert!

Now instead of being mad, find something fun, healthy, and productive to do. You were just reacting in the moment and caught up in an emotional loop. But emotional loops are like myths renting space in your brain; they don't have to be your reality. You don't have to be upset or worry each time. You learn after a while to let a lot of things go and gain more control of yourself.

When I first started practicing this point, I was mad one day at 10:30 a.m. I thought, okay, that's it. I am mad about that. I am definitely making that my mad moment tomorrow at 9 a.m. Then I thought, wait, it's 10:30. I was supposed to be mad at 9 a.m. today about yesterday. I forgot! Then I realized that these emotions are not absolutes. If I reschedule them to another day I can stay free of these darn emotional traps. I can stay connected with my healthy self.

4. Limit how much time you spend on any problem.

Schedule a limited amount of time each day when you will deal with big tasks or problems you don't enjoy. For example, spend 15 minutes evaluating the situation and make the best decision possible at the moment. Often, you will do more in less time. You don't need to drain yourself. Make work efficient by making decisions and moving on. If you need more time, decide to look at it again tomorrow or some other time in the future. Don't stew over it until you are mentally and emotionally exhausted. Less *is* more.

The universe has a lot of space between galaxies for a reason; give yourself some space too. When you do, you allow your logical brain time to process without worry. Then, immediately reward yourself with a brief activity that energizes you for making a healthy decision before you go to the next task. Keep rebooting your focus and energy by looking forward to the next positive activity in your day. Much like when dieting, you should always have your next meal or snack planned.

Another helpful strategy is to manage your emotional energy. Do so by exerting your energy in steps similar to those needed for a court trial. First there is a pretrial hearing, then discovery, possibly mediation, and then the trial itself. Afterwards, a verdict is reached. Finally, if needed, sentencing is determined. Separate your big problems into parts and retain energy for each part. Everything doesn't have to happen in one day. Deal with the parts in a limited and decisive manner and get back to enjoying life. As you make decisions on each part, you will trigger good chemicals such as endorphins, dopamine, and serotonin that give you positive feelings and energy. Grinding things out only burns energy and creates stressful chemicals like adrenaline that wear you down. You can choose actions that help you stay calm and productive regardless of external circumstances.

For example, if you get upset with someone, tell them you are upset and why. But don't feel you have to take action at that moment. Once you share your concern, reboot your thoughts and immediately look for some healthy action to reward yourself for speaking up and not reacting. You will be limiting your instinctive reactions, and you will give yourself time and space to act on a healthy thought instead. That's two positive changes for the effort of one!

5. Identity the best and worst energy times of your day.

 Identify when you feel your best each day, when you naturally have your best energy. It might be 6:30 to 7 a.m., or 2 to 3 p.m.

Spend some of the time when you feel freshest, whether one minute, 15 minutes, or a half-hour *for you*—not your kids, spouse, boss, or anyone else. Do some little thing that makes you feel like *you've really lived today!* And when you are done think to yourself, that was great, and I can't wait to do it again tomorrow.

Now you can go spend the rest of your 23 hours and 59 minutes on tasks, family, others, etc. *Not doing this every day denies giving your best to yourself.* If you don't give your best to yourself you will eventually be unfulfilled and drained, which will lead you to develop an unhealthy attitude.

At first, you may have to spend that time thinking about what would make you feel as though you really lived today. Perhaps you've never given yourself permission to do something for yourself at your best time of day. Make a list and try a few things. If your initial list doesn't ring your bell, don't worry about it, just try something different until you find something that gives you joy. Don't give up until you find it. It's okay to change what works for you after a while, too. Create themes. This quarter I am going to listen to songs, or play an instrument, or just sit on the patio and watch the sun come up. This time is just for you.

At your *worst time of day* when you are sluggish and have low energy levels, don't do stressful activities, take on big tasks, or address disagreements with anyone. Instead do things that *feed your* energy. You don't have the energy to deal with critical stressors at that time, so schedule serious decisions and discussions and handling difficulties for another time. Make your low-energy time of day a free time, like recess in school.

Instead, do little things that feed you energy; eat a bite of dark chocolate, listen to a song, write a thank you note, clean off a part of your desk, or step outside and look at the flowers and feel the sunshine on your face.

When an important problem comes up during your worst time of day, acknowledge the problem and think for a moment about what has to be done right now. Then make a decision about when to address it, and go back to feeding yourself energy.

People can usually recognize their best and lowest energy points of the day, but haven't thought about how it affects them. Incorporating these practices will give you *two times a day* that you can look forward to and enjoy being you. In addition, you can create little moments throughout your day to reboot. Take a minute when the minute hand of the clock strikes the top of the hour to breathe and reflect on your best time of day, or what you will do tomorrow at your best time. Take a minute to dream or plan your next vacation or fun activity. Taking this time to reboot will break the stress cycle of the instinctive mind (which runs 24/7) and switch your thoughts over to your conscious mind.

It is amazing to hear people identify that one thing that makes them truly happy, and realize that no one is going to do this for them. You have to make a point to enjoy your best time of day by doing something just for you.

Not giving yourself what feeds your mind, body, and spirit at these times means you are denying yourself (and others) your best. Why would you want to do that? Over time that will create stress and you will resort to unhealthy coping mechanisms. Give yourself your best every day, if only for a few minutes. Look forward to enjoying that time.

Summary of Best and Worst Times of Day

• Do something that says *you really lived today*, and know that you are going to do it again tomorrow! Make it a priority to use your *best energy* for your own betterment instead of giving that time to others (spouse, kids, boss, or anyone else). This isn't selfish; others will benefit from you being the best version of you. No matter how simple, do something you love on purpose!

• Minimize your exertion at your *low energy* time of day and instead feed yourself energy. You don't have energy for battles or big tasks, instead do little activities to renew your energy and make you feel good.

• Now you have two times during the day to look forward to. This will help you to be more peaceful and in balance with yourself.

• Recognize how these cycles affect others. When you aren't calm, others become stressed when they interact with you.

Let's look at examples of daily energy timelines for two people.

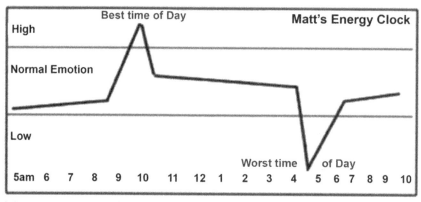

Morning Matt peaks at 10:00 a.m., then crashes at 4:30 p.m.

Morning Matt's energy is good when he wakes up, and peaks at 10 a.m. By 4:30 p.m. he is at his lowest energy level for a while, but then bounces back after dinner. Matt can be productive during his low-energy period, but should avoid taking on challenging tasks for 30 minutes or so.

At your low time of day you shouldn't tackle big issues, get into disagreements, or exert tons of energy because you just don't have sufficient energy. Instead do things that feed you energy, such as call a friend, clean off your desk, listen to music, grab a snack, play with the dog, or spend time with family.

Sample 2

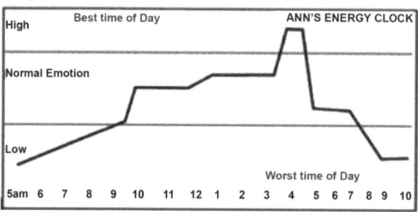

Afternoon Ann starts slow and peaks at 4:30 p.m., then falls into exhaustion after dinner.

Afternoon Ann is not a morning person. She gets off to a slow start each day getting kids off to school, and then goes in to work. She reaches peak energy later in the afternoon when all those tasks are completed. By evening she is spent.

Now imagine if morning Matt and afternoon Ann were married. They each have a different peak and low time of day. When he is ready to roll, she is just getting up to par. When she is energized, he is zonked. He rebounds in the evening, but she is exhausted. So how can they enjoy each other, date, and have serious discussions to solve problems? They can, but they have to be intentional and manage their individual energy levels daily. They need to learn not to react impulsively to their emotions, and to be more aware of their mate's needs. Life is much easier when you understand your own and your mate's daily energy cycles, and plan your interactions and time together accordingly. We would love it if our mate just knew what we need, but that isn't always the case. Bringing out the best in one another takes open communication and conscious effort.

Set your expectations with energy levels in mind. Learn what to do and what not to do at certain times. Don't react because your computer sends an emotional Alert! Create better ways to communicate as your energy levels fluctuate. For example, when you mate is feeling sluggish, lead with compliments. You might say, "I like the room arrangement you did," or "I'm looking forward to our next vacation. We had so much fun last time." When your mate is raring to go, support them by making plans to do something together. Don't be a naysayer, telling them you don't want to go out right now.

Make a calendar of your day. Schedule your best energy time on it, and your worst energy time. Make those two your most important personal times. Then schedule your work hours. Identify when you will deal with big issues, and for how long. Limit that time; make a decision and move to the next item. Reboot throughout your day with energizing thoughts or small actions that give you energy, especially after a difficult task. Reward yourself for not overreacting.

Schedule time in your day, maybe 15-20 minutes, for interruptions. Most of us have them. So allow time for them. If they don't happen, you end up with free time. Mark your family time on your calendar too, along with your social engagements and community service. The point isn't to fill your calendar, but to keep you balanced. You might choose to create a weekly calendar on an Excel spreadsheet and color code each of these types of activities in your day. If interruptions change the schedule, move the color blocks to other time slots to keep on track.

6. Wind down your brain before going to sleep.

Create a routine before going to bed to tell your mind to shut down. Your brain is thought to work harder when you sleep than during the day. During the day you gather information. At night you transfer that information from temporary storage to permanent storage. If you go to bed worrying you hinder your ability to go into the cycles that give you deep rest and a smooth transfer of mental data. Avoid watching TV or listening to music just before sleeping. Electronics stimulate the brain and emotions. Many people feel they have to use electronics, but they steal real rest. Read, play Sudoku, do puzzles, or enjoy something else that doesn't require an electronic device. Allow your mind to wind down. Learn to like hearing your own thoughts, and to be calm without outside stimulation.

Nighttime is for you to rest and be worry-free. Tell yourself your worries and concerns will be there tomorrow, and you will be more refreshed to address them after a good night's sleep anyway. If you will give up lying in bed worrying, you will have three times each day to enjoy; your peak energy time, your low energy time, and when you sleep. Focus on winding down for sleep, and tell yourself there is no need to gear up until after some specific activity, such as washing your coffee cup. Learn to be content without trying to resolve everything going on in your world in your down time. Give yourself permission to be calm and sleep.

You will still think, but you will think differently. You will reflect, not worry. You will be aware, but not stressed out. Try just sitting outside and observing what you see. Jot down the little things you notice for 20 minutes. (If you can't do this it may be an indicator you are too busy to connect with your true self.) Sit at the same spot three times in a week at the same time, writing down what you observe each time. After three times, compare your notes from each day. Notice what you miss just because you are too busy to stop and pay attention.

If you are missing the obvious things happening in nature all around you, imagine the intangible things you may be missing in your relationships. It has been noted there is more going on in the three-foot circle around you than in giant pockets of space in the universe.

7. Practice having a calm, assertive mindset.

This may seem like an odd suggestion, but Cesar Millan, also known as the "dog whisperer," has a calm, assertive technique with dogs that can benefit us humans as well. He teaches dog owners how to change the dog's state from anxious, stressed, and fearful to calm and submissive. And he shows them how to do it without words! The problem isn't the dog as much as the owner, and the leadership the dog is experiencing from its owner. Trust comes from being with a calm, assertive leader. Seeing the misbehaving dogs change their behaviors so quickly is truly amazing. Become a calm assertive leader of yourself.

At a holiday gathering I attended, the homeowner greeted me and told me to make myself at home. "Just don't touch the dog. Leave her alone and she will leave you alone," he said. I grabbed some food and sat at the end of the couch. Later, I went to the restroom, and when I returned the dog was on the couch in my seat! I knew from watching Cesar Millan that he was claiming my space as a show of authority over me. So I used Cesar's technique—no touch, no talk, and no eye contact. I simply turned my back to the dog and slowly took three steps back to my seat and went to sit down, acting as if the dog wasn't there. The dog got up and moved. The owner was watching and asked me, "How did you do that? That has never happened before." I replied, "I am the pack leader."

The same principle applies to working with people, because although people are more complex, they still have animal instincts. Your leadership can guide others to be calm and receptive as they respond to your actions. Practice it first with dogs, changing your own behaviors and experience the simplicity of the power of body language (because dogs don't speak human languages). Cesar says not to pay attention to the size of the animal, but rather pay attention to the energy they are sending out. I tell employees to apply this to anyone who has authority. Be aware of their energy, and then demonstrate calm and confidence. The authority figure will feel your energy.

Instead of being nervous and saying uh oh, here comes the boss, be ready to say something productive such as, "I wanted to let you know that one of our surgeons was complimenting you regarding the floor renovations." (Don't make up a story, just be bold enough to speak as though you belong in the conversation). Speaking to them in this way moves their thoughts to a productive part of the brain and they associate you with that memory.

"Be calm assertive - not assertive calm." Cesar Milan

Cesar means to make sure you are calm before you assert yourself. You will not get desired results if you are assertive before you are calm, because you will trigger the other person's fight, flight or freeze response.

8. Be aware of your body language; it speaks before you do.

Use your body language to sell the message you want to communicate before you start talking. So often problems can be prevented or corrected just by adopting the right posture or movement. You can even use your body language to help manage your own thoughts and emotions. When you are stressed, keep an open posture with your limbs, don't clench your fists, stand up straight, breathe slowly through your nose (not your mouth), and if you can, step outside for a moment. Focus on something energizing or imagine a scene that makes you smile. When you want to calm someone else who is stressed, speak more slowly and

114

softly than usual. Subtle actions can help significantly and bring about desired changes without using a lot of energy.

There is so much to learn about body language. Do a search online and become a student of people's body language. Observing alone is powerful and will change your attitude. Becoming aware and deliberate makes you more effective.

A client called me for help with a director who would chew people out in the hallway. Something had to be done and they wanted a suggestion right away. I knew the other directors had milder demeanors so I suggested that when the upset director started ranting that they just turn their body to block the negative energy. "That's it?," the caller asked in disbelief. I said, "Well I know the staff doesn't want to get caught up in an argument, so let them respond without words. Four hours later she called me back to thank me. She said they did as I had suggested and immediately the ranting director recognized how people were responding to her and said, "I'm sorry, did I come on too strong?" It was great to give the staff the power to resolve a problem so efficiently. It was also great the ranting director was able to use other's body language to catch herself and change her tone. Make sure your body is communicating what you want before you open your mouth.

9. Change one thing in your day.

Change one action in your day. Just focus on one change you will implement at a specific time every day or even better, several times a day. Once you see the difference you can add another.

Examples:

- Look in the mirror and tell yourself eye-to-eye that you are lovable.
- Stop eating one unhealthy food.

- Eat half-meal portions from now on. You won't likely go hungry, and you can eat the other half later in the day. You won't have missed out!
- Change one routine. Put your phone in the glove box when you drive.
- Exercise for only five minutes (often getting started is the hardest part).
- Compliment others when you greet them.
- Limit the amount of time you allow yourself to feel stress.
- Fast forward to one year from today. Look back at today from that vantage point, then, decide what is most important for you to do as a priority.

These are just a few examples. When completing the *Managing Your Crazy Self Workbook*, you will learn to solve a problem by taking one action that will help you achieves a new success at the same time. It's one step that brings a two-for-one success. Solving a problem helps, but doesn't propel you forward to real success. Achieving a goal is great, but not addressing problems will eventually catch up with you, and is essentially self-sabotage. Doing both in one step addresses both the instinctive brain and the conscious mind together. It also builds confidence and resolves emotional wounds. Once you gain that confidence, you will see problems from a different, healthier point of view.

I wanted to lose weight and learned that losing a pound a week requires burning 3,500 calories more than I eat. Breaking that down over a week meant I needed to save or burn an average of 500 calories a day. So I started eating half portions of meals. I was amazed how that simple change cut my daily caloric intake. I think I eat fairly healthfully (don't we all); I just eat too much. I started ordering whatever I wanted when eating out, or filling my plate as I normally would at home. Then I would put half the food in a to-go box. I still get to eat it, just two hours later. I call it grazing, instead of wolfing down my food before I even know how much I ate. At first I would often eat the whole hamburger and be upset I didn't cut it in half. But I didn't beat myself up. I just kept committing to eat only half the next time. The secret is to ask for a to-go box before you start eating. Then you can put half of your meal in the to-go box and enjoy every bite of what remains on the plate.

Changing this one action helped me stop overeating. I learned to be a little hungry after a meal, but looked forward to eating the rest in two to three hours. I lost the weight I wanted to and now eating less is a lifestyle for me, not a diet.

10. Do one *great thing* each day!

On your weekly or monthly calendar, write down one great thing you did that day. At the end of a week, review the calendar to see if you did seven great things. If not, don't beat yourself up. Just say, hmm, I only got one great thing in last week. I need to get three in this week. Just make the next week a little better. Remember you have to repeat the cycle of thinking and doing until you reap the desired results of your new habit.

11. Realize you are always talking to the other person's instinctive brain.

Because the instinctive brain is always running in all of us, realize you are always talking to the other person's instinctive brain. You may wish you were talking to their conscious mind, but their instinctive brain is listening to and observing everything going on. Learn to choose your words and actions to lead them to think with their conscious mind and avoid triggering their instinctive brain to react unnecessarily.

The reason bullying is so damaging is that it triggers the other person's fight, flight, or freeze thinking and blocks access to the confidence they can only get from their conscious mind. Antagonists will use this method to keep people off their game.

Instead of verbally attacking someone, speak honestly about the consequences of their behavior. For example, you might say, "If you continue to be late, that action will require being written up." Don't say "I will have to write you up," because that sounds like you are the problem instead of their tardiness. Do say

"...will require writing that action up" instead of "...write you up." Separate the action from the person.

Remember that your instinctive brain will not naturally compliment you. It's only job is to seek and find the next worry or danger to warn you about. This is why it is so important to use your conscious mind to say affirming things to yourself and others. Look in the mirror and, in the words of Billy Crystal, tell yourself, "You look marvelous!" Many people find that their instinctive brain will try to combat even a compliment by dismissing it as invalid. Don't let the ostrich control you! Be a rhino and take charge by accepting compliments and giving them to others often.

12. Ask yourself "Who said?"

One of the early illustrations in the book shows the ostrich asking "Who said...?" When you feel stress, anxiety, anger, sadness, or any other powerful negative emotion ask yourself, "Who told me to feel this way? Who said?" Ultimately, you did. Explore why your feelings rise like they do. Why get upset like you do? Why not just be aware? Decide on some other steps to do instead of getting all worked up.

That discouraging comment that runs a continuous loop in your brain may have come from someone else, but you bought into it (allowed it to affect you) and allowed it to develop into a habit of thinking. That was then. Now, however, you can choose to feel differently. When you acknowledge you are the authority who said you should feel a certain way, you can correct your perception by telling yourself you are not required to think that way. Making this choice frees you from your past perception. Now you have to decide what you will do instead. Ask yourself: How can I be okay if I don't get what I want?

Instead of reacting to stress by thinking, "Ugh, I have so much to do," tell yourself that you'll have to deal with that Tuesday at 4:15 p.m. and that right now you need a short nap. Or take a moment to write a thank you note or two. Making good decisions moves thoughts into the neocortex and stops the panic and stress. An added benefit is that you will deal with the situation that stressed you out more efficiently later on.

As you try each of these rhino tips, remember that you will experience three stages in the process.

Three stages you experience while making changes in your behaviors:

1. First, think it, until you do it. You have to be aware enough to catch yourself falling into old habits and remember what you want to do instead. Don't beat yourself up when you mess up. Realize that spotting the old habits is part of learning to change. Commit to keep working at it because the new you is coming.

2. Second, do it until it becomes a habit. Eventually, you will do it without thinking about it! You will wonder how you ever managed doing it the old way.

3. Third, listen. At some point, others will notice and give you feedback acknowledging the change they see in you. This is when you know you are mastering the change.

Realize that others may notice your new actions for some time before they say anything. That is okay, too. Others will say something right off the bat, such as when you are dieting, "Your face looks thinner. You are looking good."

When you do implement your new changes, your instinctive brain will record them and slowly build trust that they are okay in your memory. As a result, you will eventually catch yourself doing your old habit and not like it. It will happen like sand filling one side of the scales. One day the scale will tip to the other side, and you will have made a huge difference doing one little thing consistently.

Chapter 19

Summary

Put the sequence all together.
Picture converting negative thoughts to positive thoughts.

Turn down the volume of negativity.

So often you get tired of the noise in your head.

Limit the false Alerts! from your instinctive brain because they drain you.

Take Charge of Your Life

Take charge of your mind and emotions. Put your ostrich brain worries, anxiety, and stress in a canoe and send them around the bend. Otherwise, your ostrich brain will never shut up.

Goodbye worries. Finally, some peace of mind for a while.

Live the life you have always wanted to live!

Chapter 20

Resonate With People

You resonate with people when you communicate
in their style.

Making music with others!

Talk to others, adapting to their personality style, to be more
effective. Resonate with them.

Resonate with others

When you change, others will change too. They are going to have to behave differently as they react to your new behaviors. Some people may not be ready for your change in behavior because they are stuck in their instinctive brain.

When others do not improve their behavior, stay calm and strong. Find a way to help them move them to their conscious mind. Compliment them on something they did very well or that you enjoy about them. Change the setting by suggesting you go for a walk outside. Offer to help them with something.

When you strike an E chord, everything nearby with the same frequency resonates with that chord. The same principle applies to people. Strike a note or chord they connect with in their personality and they will naturally resonate with you. They will feel a natural connection with you because they feel validated and affirmed in their worth.

Chapter 21

Recognizing Your Spirit

Calm your instinctive brain to experience your spirit.

- Spirit is called spirit because it isn't physical. This means your spirit essence has nothing to do with your personality traits, physical features, culture, economics, education, and so on. Spirits have their own individual gifts, such as teaching, encouraging, mercy, service, administration, and discernment, to name a few. Your spirit is your essence. Your instinctive brain is a tool (processor) in a body. Your mind is the conscious you, capable of intentional decisions.

- Spiritual thoughts originate separately from the brain. They are received in the conscious mind first, then passed to the instinctive brain (the brain's computer that scans for danger or problems). This is how the spirit and body work in tandem.

- Thoughts from your spirit tend to feel like an intuition, a gut check, a conviction, or a knowing or understanding that you trust, even if you cannot put it into words. These thoughts can also generate emotions.

Chapter 22

Putting It All Together!

The instinctive brain, conscious mind, and spirit can work in harmony.

- the ostrich represents the instinctive brain.

- the rhino represents the conscious mind.

- the spirit rhino represents the human spirit.

All three are in each person. Understanding how each part of you works helps you to be a better version of yourself. When you add your personality traits, love language, learning style, experiences, relationships, dreams and goals, you have a clearer understanding of how to be happy and make healthy decisions that work for you.

A few key summary points

The illustration on the next page charts how information flows from your instinctive brain to the conscious mind and back. Your conscious mind and spirit also communicate back and forth. Starting on the left, your five senses bring information to your brain. When your conscious mind becomes aware of a thought, such as something you physically observe with your senses or from your spiritual nature, those thoughts are routed immediately over to the limbic system for scanning. Your limbic system then scans that information for danger, and sends Alerts! to trigger fight, flight, or freeze reactions if it perceives a problem. If there is no conscious intervention, you stay caught in those reactive behaviors until you perceive the problem is gone. This process is instinctive. You haven't done anything consciously yet.

If no problem is perceived, only then does information pass to your conscious mind. This is when you get to engage. This loop goes on all day. Calming your instinctive mind's Alerts! and not reacting allows you to embrace your conscious mind, which then communicates with your spirit.

At any time, you may naturally loop back to the instinctive brain for scanning, such as when you get a phone call or new email, when you think a new thought, or when something or someone interrupts you. The key is to stay in the conscious or spirit mind and not get caught in reactionary behaviors.

Picture the flow of thoughts and emotions.

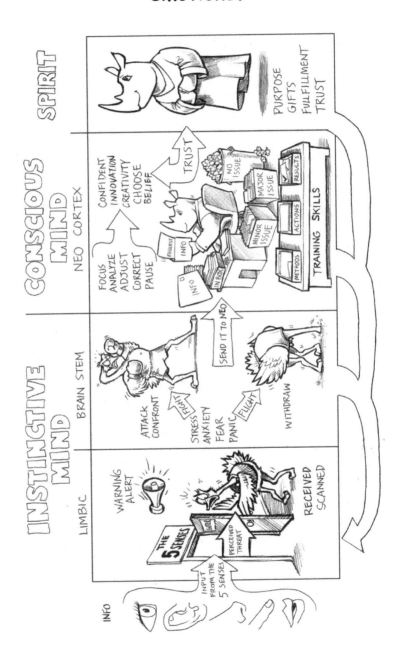

Summary Points

1. Your instinctive brain is very active long before your conscious mind kicks in. Understanding what activity is happening instinctively will help you control and manage your thoughts and emotions consciously.

2. By the time you engage conscious thoughts you will need to undo many of the thoughts and emotions from your instinctive brain. This is a healthy correction, best done using redirection. Your brain creates different thoughts and emotions depending on which area of the brain you are thinking in. You get to choose.

3. Your instinctive brain records all memories and scans them constantly to search for danger and send Alerts! to protect you from danger. It is not trying to make you upset or drive you crazy. It is always running and has to be redirected or managed continuously. Your instinctive brain is wired to be managed by your conscious mind. Give yourself permission to do so. Not doing so can make you an emotional wreck with unhealthy behaviors.

4. All thoughts begin or are rerouted to the limbic system for protective scanning. In a way, your mind thinks danger first. If you don't override your instinctive brain, you can become fearful, stressed, or immobilized. You have to choose to take chances and actions that lead to success.

5. Perceived dangers trigger Alerts! and fight, flight, or freeze reactions.

6. Your instinctive brain will not initiate complimentary thoughts and emotions. It can only accept them once your conscious mind is made aware of them.

7. The more you use your conscious mind the more you calm down the worrisome noise from your instinctive brain.

8. The instinctive brain will never tell the conscious mind how or when to take charge. You have to learn by just doing it. Use some of the methods suggested in this book to help you.

9. Continuing to react in fight, flight, or freeze will deny you the benefit of objective thinking from your conscious mind.

10. Making conscious mind decisions stops fight, flight, or freeze reactions and calms emotions. The instinctive brain will follow the lead from your conscious mind.

11. The instinctive brain is mature from birth while the conscious mind matures years later in childhood and even into adulthood. You are always growing mentally. Because your conscious mind wasn't mature when unmet expectations and emotional wounds originated, you are not usually aware of their impact as they surface later in life, usually in relationships.

12. Insecurities are stored in your instinctive brain. They are to be healed through conscious mind decisions, using new knowledge that brings light to your perceptions. These new perspectives rewrite new emotions associated with old events.

13. Thoughts and emotions recorded in childhood can go dormant for years only to surface later in new relationships. This is why post-traumatic stress happens. The war is over, but the emotions have not been dealt with in a healthy way.

14. Four key relationships where deep emotions surface are with yourself, your mate, your children, and your coworkers.

15. You can make healthy changes in your instinctive brain by better managing your behaviors and perceptions in your relationships.

16. Build practices and methods into your day that help you redirect unhelpful thoughts and emotions to something fun

and enjoyable, which will help you manage your behaviors. You will reduce stress in your life.

17. When you change, others change too, because they respond to your actions.

18. Freeing yourself from your instinctive brain will help you recognize your conscious mind and your spirit. It will also change the chemicals your brain releases into your body, often affecting different organs.

19. Your instinctive brain is only a processor; it cannot understand your spirit. Your limbic system is just processing data; it isn't a person with a will. Your instinctive brain does its job scanning what you bring it, but you are responsible to make decisions from your conscious mind.

Chapter 23

What Is Your Next Step?

Keep learning about you.

You've already taken the first step—reading this book! *Managing Your Crazy Self!* is designed to help you understand how the instinctive brain processes your experiences into thoughts and emotions, and to provide commonsense methods to take charge using your conscious mind. Taking charge of reactive emotions using your conscious mind brings peace and order to your emotions and relationships, and helps you achieve your goals. But there is so much more!

The second step is to learn how your personality dynamics are hardwired. This step reveals how your personality dynamics shape your thoughts like a prism separates colors. You determine your unique personality dynamics by completing assessments. The set of tools I use measure your behavior style, motivators, learning styles, love languages, EQ, and gifts. You can order and complete these assessments from anywhere in the North Americas by contacting me or ordering from the website www.cerosinc.com. You can learn about your results in several ways. Most people gain a lot of benefit from attending a workshop because they see how others react and respond to one another's personality dynamics. However, I often explain assessment results one-on-one over the phone or via Skype. I have coached many people with very good success over the phone, never having met them face-to-face. The assessment reports, graphs, and worksheets are in your hands while we talk, so you can hear the explanations and we each see our expressions.

We are all wired so uniquely. Even if we have the same behavior style, we have different motivators, learning styles, love languages, and gifts. We come from different cultures, socio-economic backgrounds, faiths, etc. The beauty of this step is that you will understand and use insights about your hardwiring for the rest of your life. Behavior style assessment is not a fad; it's a very useful graph of how your brain processes daily life. Each assessment type measures different aspects that make you uniquely you as outlined below.

Behavior style: Measures *how* you perceive problems, people, procedures, and pace of daily life. You cannot escape your behavior style. It is the core software to your brain and determines how you display your other personality traits.

Motivators: Measures *why* you are motivated, addressing theoretical, utilitarian, aesthetic, social, individualistic, and traditional drives. This tool captures the powerful undercurrent driving your behavior.

Learning styles: Measures the best way to present new information to you so you can absorb it, whether visual, auditory, or experiential. If you are auditory and need to hear or talk about new concepts, then written instructions or a written job description won't help you learn very effectively.

Love languages: Measures how you want to be appreciated, with words, touch, service, things (gifts), or quality time. If your love language is words and people give you gifts, you will tend to view the gifts as dust collectors. The gifts may even feel more like an added chore, rather than an expression of appreciation.

Emotional Intelligence (EQ): Measures your emotional and social intelligence in your interactions with other people. Factors include self-awareness, self-regulation, motivators, empathy, and social skills as compared to others. EQ is not a genetic; you can improve your EQ.

Gifts: Measures your primary expressions of human spirit, the areas where you find your greatest fulfillment. There are many gifts but nine that are commonly acknowledged are declaring truth, teaching, encouraging, service, mercy, giving, administration, leading, and recruiting. Your other personality dynamics have

134

more to do with how you process life whereas as these expressions are ways you are most likely to find real fulfillment.

The third step is to complete the *Managing Your Crazy Self Workbook*. The workbook will help you address where you've been, where you are now, and where you want to go. You will create a visual representation of your past, present, and future and determine your priorities moving forward. This exercise is very personal to you, and will give you a deep understanding of your perceptions and shed light on the course corrections you most want and need.

The fourth step is coaching. Most people require interaction with a skilled coach to make sense of the patterns in their lives and pinpoint the next steps to create the life they have always desired. Coaching helps you use all the insights you've gathered throughout this process efficiently and effectively. We'll find the one key change you need to resolve the emotional driver that holds you back and to propel you to achieve with a new ease. You'll gain confidence and belief in yourself like you've never had before. The objective is to achieve maximum results with minimal effort. Understanding how your mind and personality dynamics function is critical. Coaching is also crucial, because it provides training and objective feedback, encourages you, and holds you accountable.

The fifth step is to embrace the new healthier you, connect more with your spirit, and enjoy better relationships with others. You now can achieve your potential with peace and fulfillment like never before.

Reminders

• Practice managing your instinctive brain reactions by using the following methods to move thoughts to your conscious mind.

   ✓ Tell yourself that *unhelpful emotional reactions* are NOT REQUIRED.
   ✓ NAME your crazy self (a name that makes you laugh)!
   ✓ REDIRECT negative emotions until tomorrow.

- ✓ LIMIT time addressing stressful issues; make a decision and move on.
- ✓ Give yourself PERMISSION to take a fun, healthy, productive action. Often this is something that is the opposite of your normal reactions. Compliment someone you dislike. Keep it simple, such as "I like your shoes!"
- ✓ REWARD yourself in healthy ways.

- Catch your thoughts; question them; take charge.

- Be good to yourself at least once a day!

- Learn more from the video tips, training, and coaching at www.cerosinc.com.

- Attend a Managing Your Crazy Self or Five Steps to Renew Your Mind workshop.

- Read other books by Randy Guttenberger, including *Managing Your Crazy Self Personality Dynamics,* and the *Managing Your Crazy Self Workbook*.

- Sign up for coaching with Randy. Invest in yourself and your relationships!

- Tell others! Give this book as a gift.

- Become a Ceros, Inc. distributor.

- Invite Randy to speak at your organization, work with your staff, or lead your organizational retreat.

- These principles run deep; if you continue to study them, you will continue to grow.

Need help? Contact Randy Guttenberger, Ceros, Inc.
www.cerosinc.com
randy@cerosinc.com

Appendix

Glossary of Terms

Abnormal: A fun way to say wonderfully unique! No one person has all the positive qualities every person can possess. Everyone has gaps and challenges. I like to think of it this way: humans are all abnormal because no one can have every human quality; therefore, abnormal is normal, i.e., common.

Alert!: A thought or feeling from the brain indicating potential danger that may require defensive action. Alerts are not necessarily based in reality.

Amygdala: Part of the limbic system of the brain that research has discovered performs a primary role in the processing of memory and emotional reactions. Most emotions associated with events are stored here. These emotions can be changed as you learn new information and gain a new perspective. This is the part of the brain where emotional wounds are healed.

Assessment: A tool that measures the strength or weakness of a trait as compared to others.

Brain stem: The part of the mind that responds to perceived danger with fight, flight, or freeze behaviors. The brain stem triggers chemicals such as adrenaline to make the body act quickly. Adrenaline increases your heart rate, stimulates your sweat glands, and gives your muscles energy.

Calm assertive: A mindset that is calm and not anxious. It takes action but does not react.

Calm submissive: A mindset that is calm; it follows but does not lead; it is relaxed.

Ceros: The last part of the word rhinoceros. From the Greek *rhīno* (nose) and *ceros* (horn), i.e., a horn-nosed animal.

Conscious mind: The neocortex is the cognitive or conscious part of your brain where you intentionally choose your thoughts or actions. It is often referred to as the frontal lobe.

Conviction: An intuitive or gut feeling that something is true or false. You feel an understanding or awareness in your spirit that is different from how emotions surface in your mind.

Coping mechanisms: Behaviors a person adopts to deal with stress or pain. Coping mechanisms may persist long after the source of stress or pain is gone. Unhealthy coping mechanisms have negative consequences.

DISC behavior style: DISC is an acronym for the temperament styles called Decisive, Inspiring, Steady, and Compliant. Each person has a blend of all four. One is more dominant than the others and is called an individual's core behavior style.

Dopamine: A chemical the body produces that creates a high or energized feeling in response to anticipation. Thinking about something good, smelling chocolate cookies, or taking food or drugs into your body can create dopamine.

Dynamics: The forces of various personality traits that affect interactions between people.

False self: The way you want others to perceive you that does not correspond with your true self.

Fear: An alert originating in the instinctive brain that is designed to warn us of danger. Fears can only be resolved with the cognitive or conscious part of our minds.

Gifts: Natural abilities such as leadership, mercy, encouraging, and teaching. Developing skills can enhance these gifts, but the gifts are always present in a person. For example, a singer can sing but may need to learn the skills needed to perform well. A painter has an innate talent or gift, but still needs to learn the craft and techniques to do his or her best work.

Guilt: A feeling or awareness of remorse for committing a wrong.

Happiness: A sense of pleasure or state of contentment. Happiness may be the result of a desire or expectation being met.

Hippocampus: Part of the limbic system of the brain. This is where memories of events are stored. When memories of events are recalled in the conscious mind, we also often recall the emotions associated with those events. The memories of the events will not change, but the emotions associated with particular events are stored in a different place (the amygdala), and can be changed.

Imago: A term coined by Harville Hendrix to represent the conception of our ideal mate that we create in our minds. This ideal is a combination of the good traits you see in the person, the good traits you saw in your parents, traits you consciously determined you want in a mate, and possibly some positive traits you saw in other people. The imago is a fictitious image that can never be lived up to by a real person; it is an unrealistic expectation.

Instinctive brain: The subconscious mind where thoughts, feelings, and actions are initiated before you willingly choose to act. The limbic system and brain stem make up the instinctive part of the brain.

Lost self: A term coined by author Harville Hendrix, the lost self is the part of ourselves that we have hidden from our conscious minds in response to messages we received in childhood that something about us was not acceptable or desirable.

Limbic system: The deep-rooted 5% of the mind that stores our memories and emotions. The limbic system scans current activity from our five senses and compares it to past events searching for danger or problems.

Methods: Practical actions that help you manage emotions and problems effectively and efficiently.

Mind: The mind is made up of three key parts: the limbic system, the brain stem, and the neocortex. Each part has a different function and can act independently of the others, though they often relate to and affect each other.

Motivators: The drivers that stimulate you to act. The assessment tool I use and recommend categorizes people into six primary categories of motivation: theoreticals love learning; utilitarians make things function; aesthetics appreciate the setting; socials care for others; individualistic types want to achieve; and traditionals believe in the cause.

Neocortex: The part of our brain that controls our cognitive mind, where reasoning occurs. The neocortex is where we choose our thoughts and actions, and where belief, trust, innovation, and creativity originate.

Pack leader: The alpha or top dog in a pack of dogs; the leader of the group.

Principle: A general concept determined to be a truth or a consistent description of reality. Reality includes forces that shape our experience of life. A principle is based on observation of how things work, including how people interact with one another because of those forces.

Renew: Reenergize or rework with new information. Reboot. Revive. Give yourself a fresh start.

Serotonin: One of the chemicals the body produces that gives us pleasure or a feeling of "ahhhhh."

Shame: Feeling bad about who you are; having a sense that you are a bad person. This is different from guilt, which is feeling bad about something you have done.

Trigger: Something that sets off your emotions and leads you to react.

Will: The power the mind has to make purposeful decisions; a determination of belief or course of action.

Worth: In this book, the word "worth" refers to self-worth, which is how you value yourself.

Fun Facts about the Ostrich

- Genus and species: *Struthio camelus;* family: Struthionidae

- Ostriches have been around for 120 million years. Wild African black ostriches are found only in sub-Saharan Africa; however, they can be found in captivity all over the world.

- An ostrich is the largest living bird today, standing about nine feet tall.

- The ostrich has a nasty temper.

- They do not actually bury their heads in the ground. They lay their necks along the ground when they sleep, which can give the impression that their heads are in the ground.

- An ostrich can run up to 40 miles per hour for extended time, though they tend to run in circles when avoiding predators.

- An ostrich fights with its feet, and can kick a lion to death. They have only two toes on each foot, and they kick forward because of their knee structure.

- Each ostrich eyeball is bigger than its brain, with the eyes taking up most of the space in their skull.

- Ostriches are omnivorous, eating both vegetation and meat. They have been known to eat most anything, including man-made items such as alarm clocks and small bottles.

- They don't have to drink water, but they will if it is available.

- The ostrich egg is the largest of all eggs. It has a volume equal to two dozen chicken eggs.

- A baby ostrich grows one foot in height per month the first seven months of its life.

- Ostriches produce the strongest commercially available leather.

These fun facts were adapted from the following sources:

http://animals.howstuffworks.com/birds/ostrich-facts.htm

http://www.livescience.com/27433-ostriches.html

Fun Facts about Rhinos

- Family: Rhinocerotidae. There are five species of rhinos today: white, black, Sumatran, Indian, and Javan. Three of the species are from southern Asia, and two are from Africa.

- The black, Javan, and Sumatran are on the critically endangered list with only about 29,000 extant in the wild.

- The word rhinoceros is of Greek origin; *rhīno* meaning "nose" and *ceros* meaning "horn." Some rhinoceroses have one horn, and others have two, they are often hunted for their horns.

- The Sumatran rhino emerged about 50 million years ago.

- Rhinos are known to charge when they feel threatened.

- Rhinos have poor eyesight, but great hearing and sense of smell.

- Rhinos have thick skin, but it is sensitive to insects and sun.

- Rhinos are mostly solitary, but some do travel in families.

- Rhino horns are made of a protein called keratin, the same substance as fingernails.

- A group of rhinos is called a crash.

- Rhinos can run 30 to 40 miles per hour.

- Rhinos have lived on every continent except South America and Australia.

- Rhinos can grow over six feet high and eleven feet long. The largest white rhino can weigh over 5,000 pounds, second in size only to the elephant.

- Rhinos are herbivores, eating only plants.

- Oxpecker birds hang out with rhinos to eat bugs off their backs, and they screech when sensing danger.

These fun facts were adapted from the following sources:

https://www.savetherhino.org/rhino_info/for_kids/everything_rhino

http://www.livescience.com/27439-rhinos.html

Bibliography

Crawford, Bill, PhD. *Life from the Top of the Mind.* Houston: Florence Publishing, 2006.

Brown, Elizabeth B. *Living Successfully with Screwed Up People.* Grand Rapids, MI: Revell, 1999.

Hendrix, Harville, PhD. *Getting the Love you Want: A Guide for Couples,* 20th anniversary edition. New York: St. Martin's Press, 2008.

Bradshaw, John. *Bradshaw on: The Family: A New Way of Creating Solid Self-Esteem.* Deerfield Beach, FL: Health Communications, 1988.

Bennett-Goleman, Tara. *Emotional Alchemy: How the Mind Can Heal the Heart.* New York: Three Rivers Press, 2001.

Bonnstetter, Bill J., Judy I. Suiter, and Randy J. Widrick. *The Universal Language of DISC.* Scottsdale, AZ: Target Training International, 1993.

Additional Reading

Chapman, Gary. *The Five Love Languages: The Secret to Love That Lasts.* Chicago: Northfield Publishing, 2004.

Leaf, Dr. Caroline. *Who Switched Off My Brain?: Controlling Toxic Thoughts and Emotions.* Southlake, TX: InProv Limited, 2009.

About the Author

Randy Guttenberger is a Certified Professional Behavioral Analyst, in Houston, Texas, where he has been active in his executive coaching business, Ceros, Inc., since 1996. Before that, he worked for eleven years as an executive with the Boy Scouts of America in Houston.

Randy left scouting to pursue his vision of bringing tools and insights to people to help them succeed. He felt so many people were not aware of the great tools he had been privileged to utilize. As a behavioral analyst, Randy helps you resolve the issues you don't know you have that cause the relationship or success problems you do know you have.

He created *What You're Good At*, a student career assessment program and workbook, in 1996. The program used corporate assessments to help students understand how they addressed problems, people, procedures, and pace of the day and to identify their motivators to help them find careers that fit their personality. The program guided students to prioritize and vet their career possibilities, find universities that matched their career list, and network with professionals to have a job when they graduated. Randy was soon invited by parents of students to work with their companies. Parents said if he could identify dynamics of their high school student so accurately without ever having met them, he could likely help executives in their company.

After years of success proving the concepts in coaching, Randy committed to write down the principles of how the mind, personality dynamics, and experiences affect individuals and their relationships. The result is three books addressing the mind, personality traits, and experiences: *Managing Your Crazy Self,* *Managing Your Crazy Self Personality Dynamics,* and the *Managing Your Crazy Self Workbook.* Randy also trains coaches to help clients apply these principles to their lives.

Today Randy speaks, coaches professionals and families, produces audio and video podcasts, creates online courses, and certifies distributors to teach the *Managing Your Crazy Self!* principles. He is looking forward to writing his next book, *Living a Spiritual Life in a Physical World.*

Ceros, Inc.,
Randy Guttenberger,
Certified Professional Behavioral Analyst,
Houston, TX
randy@cerosinc.com; www.cerosinc.com

About the Illustrator

Shawn K. Carson has illustrated seven books, including *The Zabbit* and T*he Slice of Swiss Cheese from Switzerland*. He has been teaching art for over three decades and now owns Carson's Art School in Katy, Texas. His latest project is an online program to help more struggling artists discover their true potential. He loves creating portraits and cartoons along with many other styles of art. This versatility helps bring to life his client's visions and concepts. You can see more of his art at shawnkcarson.com .

Illustrating this book series by Randy Guttenberger has been particularly rewarding for Shawn not only because of the fun nature of the artwork, but because his drawings can engage the reader in a way that helps make Randy's message more clear and memorable. Shawn knows firsthand how the principles in this book can change lives dramatically, delivering powerful concepts in a fun and understandable way. A hurting or confused person can receive that revelation they have been blind to for years, paving the way for real, lasting change. Shawn's family has been personally affected by the stress of wrong thinking and he hopes his art can help broken minds, hearts, and souls begin to heal.

www.shawnkcarson.com